ARCHITECTURE
THE GROUNDBREAKING MOMENTS

ARCHITECTURE
THE GROUNDBREAKING MOMENTS

ISABEL KUHL

PRESTEL
Munich · London · New York

CONTENT

INTRODUCTION

What do the Egyptian pyramids, St. Peter's Basilica in Rome, and the Guggenheim Museum in Bilbao, Spain have in common? Not much, you would think. After all, these buildings have completely different functions and historically they are separated by centuries or even millennia.

However, they do have one important thing in common. They all bear witness to groundbreaking moments in architecture, which still resonate today and which have opened up new directions for architecture itself. The controversial glass Louvre Pyramid, built in the last century, is based on the model to be found in Giza in Egypt, which is four and a half thousand years older. With St. Peter's, the greatest church in Christendom, the architects of the sixteenth and seventeenth centuries ushered in the Baroque period; and the high-tech architecture of the branch of the Guggenheim in Bilbao in the Basque region of Spain has made it a new travel destination for many people.

This is the timeframe defined by the architectural ideas presented in this book—a journey from the ancient Egyptians to the architects of today. We have chosen 20 themes which had and still have major consequences for architecture. These 20 chapters look at individual building projects, technical achievements, or materials which have taken architecture in a new direction. Classical architectural masterpieces are given priority, but we will also be looking at lesser-known projects as well.

The book is organized chronologically. After the pyramids come the classical orders, whose importance will become clear through the example of the Greek temples, and which we will follow into the nineteenth century. Other chapters are devoted to the building of domes, and to architecture on paper—that is, the architectural plan. Church building, a task which was so important to Western architecture, comes up many times in our journey through groundbreaking moments. Church architects in the Middle Ages already preferred the longitudinal ground-plan of the basilica form, and so we have devoted a chapter to this type of building. At the same time the late Middle Ages, the Gothic period, is also the era of the great cathedrals. These often enormous churches could be built as a result of major advances in construction: buttressing and pointed arches are responsible for the characteristically mountainous profiles of Gothic architecture—and as a result they are the main focus of the chapter on cathedrals.

left—**MICHELANGELO, NEW SACRISTY OF SAN LORENZO** | Florence 1520–34 | view of the ceiling.

The historical and intellectual foundations of an era are not central to our discussion. But as the understanding of architecture is often extremely difficult without any knowledge of them, we will at least mention them. This is our also approach to the architecture of the Renaissance and the Baroque, which will be presented starting with their origins in Florence and Rome. Equally, some architectural challenges which faced architects over the course of the centuries, such as the magnificent palaces of the Baroque, as well the spectacular skyscrapers of the twentieth century, are the subject of individual chapters.

And on the subject of skyscrapers, the high-rise building is the moment when glass and steel come into play. All building work was dominated by wood and stone until well into the eighteenth century. But after that the vocabulary of architecture broadened considerably in the space of just two hundred years. We reflect this development in individual chapters, showing how the use of glass in architecture benefited from the development of cast iron. And we discuss the twentieth century as the age of concrete, which opened up completely new possibilities. A comparatively weightless material—light—still fascinates architects today and so building with light will also be a central topic.

We will also be looking at different architectural movements. The belief that form must respond to the function of a building found its way onto the drawing board for the first time through the advocates of Functionalism after World War I. The idea that technology should determine the form of a house was once more an approach that the High-Tech architects of the 1970s espoused. Finally we look at the Deconstructivists, who were responsible for dismantling every single accepted idea about architecture. Twenty ideas that had an impact on the history of architecture are waiting to be discovered in this book. Other architectural innovations and masterworks remain necessarily on the margins: for example, the architecture of the English Baroque looks quite different from the Italian version; and the pyramids of Central America are no less interesting than their Egyptian cousins. There are so many fascinating architectural projects—if we don't have room to mention them in these pages it doesn't mean they are not worth further investigation.

In our architectural journey there is one person who we discuss relatively rarely—and that is the architect himself or herself. This contradiction can be explained by the architect's role in society. Until well into the Middle Ages a building project was associated more with the work's patron than with the architect who worked on it. Only rarely do we get to know anything about the latter. The freelance, artistic creative architect is a quite recent notion, which only came about during the fifteenth century at the time of the Italian Renaissance.

The basis for the understanding of the architect's role was established in the first century B.C. by the Roman architect Vitruvius. His ten-volume work, *De Architectura*, is the oldest surviving text on the subject. For Vitruvius, creative talent based on knowledge was what went into the making of an architect, as he wrote: "In fact, all kinds of men, and not merely architects, can recognize a good piece of work, but between laymen and the latter there is this difference, that the layman cannot tell what it is to be like without seeing it finished, whereas the architect, as

soon as he has formed the conception, and before he begins the work, has a definite idea of the beauty, the convenience, and the propriety that will distinguish it." It was only with the arrival of the Renaissance that Vitruvius's writings would achieve their full impact. Until that time architects were considered craftsmen. But from the thirteenth century onwards we begin to recognize their names more and more frequently on documents, bills of sale, or inscriptions. Occasionally they moved around from one building site to another, in demand as experts, and thus they disseminated their architectural knowledge. But their importance in society only changed during the Renaissance. Many architects in the fifteenth and sixteenth centuries were artists who were given building projects as a result of their talent for invention. Filippo Brunelleschi was one of the first universal men of this period, and his achievements heralded the beginning of Renaissance architecture itself. His contemporary, Leon Battista Alberti, approached architecture in the light of Vitruvius's treatise on the subject, even showing interest in its theory, and in 1452 he published his own influential work *De re aedificatoria* [On the Art of Building in Ten Books]. With Brunelleschi and Alberti the new position of architect was introduced, and thanks to the scientific underpinning of architecture they were now considered scholars, and no longer just craftsmen. An example of this recognition by society in the centuries that followed as well is the Baroque architect Sir Christopher Wren, who was a high-ranking member of the court of King Charles II of England. Architecture established itself as an academic discipline in France at the time of the absolute monarchs. The first theoretical lectures on building appeared towards the end of the eighteenth century, when architecture had secured its position as a subject in its own right. Radical changes appeared in the nineteenth century with the advent of iron construction. A new material, new building projects, and with them new technical challenges ultimately brought about the separation of the architect, who created the design, and the engineer, who was in charge of construction. The latter became a specialist in the technical and scientific fields and took over the construction aspect of building.

Whether it is made of iron or stone, whether its builder is anonymous, a celebrated architectural genius, or a daring engineer, every building is based on an idea. And it is some of these exciting architectural ideas which we explore in this book of groundbreaking moments.

above—HERZOG & DE MEURON, BEIJING NATIONAL STADIUM | 2008.

c. 2890 BC—Beginning of Dynasty II of Egypt ·· *c. 2300 BC*—End of the Old Kingdom of Egypt···

c. 2686 BC—End of Dynasty II of Egypt·······································

c. 2500 BC—Construction of the pyramids of Giza···························

10/11

c. 2800 BC Imhotep

PYRAMIDS: THE FIRST HOUSES BUILT FOR ETERNITY

The giant pyramids of Egypt were not tombs in the strict sense of the word. Rather, their builders saw them more as houses for living in after death. Over eighty of these eternal stone houses still exist in the flat landscape of the Nile valley, and they continue to fascinate us. For many years now they have also been assured a place in the vocabulary of architectural forms.

The first pyramids, huge limestone-clad buildings along the banks of the Nile, appeared in the third century B.C. The tradition of pyramid building began under the pharaohs of the Old Kingdom. The Greek historian Diodorus explained this cult in the first century B.C., writing that the Egyptians "consider the period of this life to be of no account whatever, but place the greatest value on the time after death ... and while they give the name of 'lodgings' to the dwellings of the living, ... they call the tombs of the dead 'eternal homes'." (Diodorus I, 1.60) The monumental stone structures, which can be seen for miles across the flat landscape, were by no means alone: they were part of extensive burial grounds, which were constructed for life after death.

In the third century B.C. an entire city of the dead grew up in Giza on the west bank of the Nile not far from Cairo. Several pyramids of differing heights and hundreds of tombs of high officials spread out across an area of more than one square kilometer. King Cheops created his cemetery on a rocky plateau: at 146 meters his pyramid was the highest ever built and, incidentally, also the largest built structure in the ancient world (fig. pp. 12/13). In just twenty years, from 2554 to 2531 B.C., thousands of workers piled up around 2.5 million blocks of stone to form 210 layers of stone. If we include bearers and slaves, around twenty to twenty-five thousand people were involved in the building of the Pyramid of Cheops, one percent of the entire population of Egypt at that time. Approximately five thousand stonemasons brought the necessary blocks of rock and limestone from the quarries. The sheer mountains of material, not to mention the large numbers of workers involved, provide impressive information on how the pyramids were built. Behind this, and no less impressive, was a highly developed architectural technology and excellent mathematical knowledge: the start of pyramid building was accompanied by a massive step forward in building technology. While earlier tombs in Egypt had been constructed out of clay bricks, with the pyramids stone was used as a basic building material for the first time. The transport of the huge stone

left—THE PYRAMIDS OF GIZA.

*"Around twenty to twenty-five
thousand people were involved in
the building of the Pyramid of Cheops,
one percent of the entire population
of Egypt at that time."*

c. **1350 BC**—Bust of Nefertiti is crafted .... **753 BC**—Founding of Rome···· **PYRAMIDS** 12/13

·· **776 BC**—First Olympic Games ··

left—THE PYRAMID OF CHEOPS | 2554 – 2531 BC.

blocks was in itself a major achievement, while the construction of the pyramids was only made possible at all through the development of metal tools. Last but not not least, Egyptian architects were also in a position to calculate spatial volumes and right angles or other similar problems accurately. The smooth surfaces of the sides of the pyramid emerge from the square base as unstepped triangles, which meet at the top: despite the impressive length of the edges (in the Pyramid of Cheops they measure 230 meters) the sides differ by just a few centimeters.

Cheops' tomb, the largest of the Egyptian pyramids, displays the classic elements of pyramid construction: an east-facing valley temple, which was connected to the mortuary temple at the foot of the pyramid by an ascending passage. A lower passage led from the north entrance diagonally into the heart of the building, culminating in a great hall. So-called "portcullis slabs", suspended on ropes, protected the burial chamber beyond housing the stone sarcophagus in which the embalmed body of the deceased lay. Massive stone blocks were transported deep into the pyramid's burial chamber. According to Egyptian beliefs, this chamber was to be the deceased person's home for all eternity, and so he was to be provided for accordingly. Shafts were created to allow the circulation of fresh air; burial gifts were to equip him for his long existence in the afterlife; and fresh food

14/15 PYRAMIDS .... **543 BC**—Year 0 in the Buddhist calendar .... **214 BC**—Construction of the Wall of China
·· **457 BC**—Completion of the Temple of Zeus at Olympia ·······················
······································· **292 BC**—Completion of the Colossus of Rhodes····························

c. 500 BC Phidias   *c.* 60 BC – 10 BC Vitruvius

was left for him in the mortuary temple at the foot of the pyramid. In some pyramid constructions there was even a stone sphinx standing guard over the valley temple.

Even when the era of Egyptian pyramid building was long past, this building type persisted, and pyramids have featured in the history of Western architecture ever since. The reference to Egypt was of course more obvious in the case of obelisks: these stone pillars, which often bore Egyptian hieroglyphics, were being brought back and erected in Rome even in Antiquity. But already the Ancients were also examining the pyramid as a building type. Cheops' mammoth creation was known to the Romans when Egypt was incorporated into the empire in 30 B.C. at the latest. The Romans used the pyramid form for many of their funerary monuments. One of them, the Pyramid of Cestius in Rome (fig. above), is still standing today. The second century B.C. building was located near the Porta San Paolo city gate and is modelled in its dimensions on the buildings of the Nile. Nevertheless the Pyramid of Cestius only reached a quarter of the height of the first Egyptian pyramid, the Pyramid of Cheops.

Since then there have been few epochs that boasted no pyramids at all: although knowledge of Egyptian culture was generally lost during the Middle Ages in Europe, it was rediscovered alongside many other cultures during the Renaissance. The Renaissance popes built Egyptian obelisks in Rome, a clear indication of the growing interest in Egypt. During the Baroque period elements from Egyptian architecture influenced European garden design: pyramids and obelisks appeared in aristocratic gardens and later emerged in English landscape gardens. Scientific interest in Egypt grew during the eighteenth and nineteenth centuries, as hieroglyphics were deciphered and expeditions set off for the land of the Nile. And in the twentieth century, too, the pyramid form found its advocates: the Chinese-born American architect Ieoh Ming Pei (1917–), who was commissioned to extend the exhibition spaces of the Louvre, created its new entrance in the form of a glass pyramid (fig. right). Pei too modelled his creation on the proportions of the Great Pyramid of Giza.

above—**THE PYRAMID OF CESTIUS** | Rome | 2nd century BC.
right—**I. M. PEI, LOUVRE PYRAMID** | Paris | 1985 – 89.

457 BC—Completion of the Temple of Zeus at Olympia · 411 BC—Aristophanes writes *Lysistrata* · · · **16/17**

c. 448 BC—Completion of the Athena Parthenos ·

c. 430 BC—Completion of the Statue of Zeus at Olympia · · · · · · · · · · · · · · ·

c. 500 BC Phidias

A GREEK INVENTION:
THE CLASSICAL ORDERS

For many centuries in Ancient Greece temples were the most important form of architecture. They were, after all, houses built for the gods. Gradually the temple form of a square central space surrounded by columns came to predominate. Even the most famous Greek temple, the Parthenon on the Acropolis, follows this model. When the Parthenon was built in the fifth century B.C., Athens was the political and economic center of Greece and this temple, dedicated to the goddess protector of the city, Athena, took on a suitably monumental form. We can only imagine today how the Temple of Athena was richly decorated with architectural sculpture, and how sculptures and relief friezes adorned its façades. The cult image, a huge statue of Athena, was located in the central space, the cella. The roof of the temple was supported by a whole row of columns, and the entire temple was made of white marble. Eight stone columns adorned the west-facing front of the structure, with seventeen pillars on each of the long sides (fig. left). On these massive columns lay horizontal beams and, in turn, on top of these was the temple's pediment. A central aim of the architect

left—**ICTINOS AND CALLICRATES, THE PARTHENON** | Athens
447–432 BC.

right—**THE PARTHENON** | detail.

··········· **387 BC**—Plato founds his Academy in Athens ···················· **336 BC**—Alexander the Great becomes king of Macedonia

··········· **386 BC**—The King's Peace ends the Corinthian War···········

c. 360 BC – 316 BC Lysippos

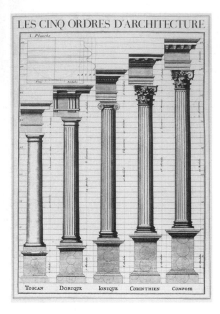

LES CINQ ORDRES D'ARCHITECTURE

TOSCAN DORIQUE IONIQUE CORINTHIEN COMPOSE

was to create a harmonious relationship between the vertical lines of the columns and the horizontal lines of the entablature above.

As in the Parthenon, columns in Greek architecture were used as supports for a horizontal entablature. They were also used not only as an architectural element, a use that refers back ultimately to the tree-trunk that was used as a support, but they were also used for their own qualities, to lend order to architecture. To do this the Greeks developed three different types of column that can be distinguished by their three sections: the base, the shaft, and most clearly by the capital that finishes the column at the top. Another element was the beams that were placed horizontally on top of the columns and that led to the pediment. The appearance of these architectural elements and what their relative proportions should be determined the classical orders as they developed in Ancient Greece. With the establishment of these three architectural forms the Greeks created an architectural principle that architects followed until well into the nineteenth century.

The plainest of the three orders is the Doric, named for the Ancient Greek tribe, the Dorians. This order was used in the building of the Parthenon. Its powerful columns have no base of their own, but stand directly on the floor of the temple. The shaft of the column tapers towards the top and is articulated

with vertical grooves, called fluting. At the top the shaft bulges out to be finished off with a covering slab, the abacus. Above the abacus are decorated lintels, and finally the pediment.

The Ionic order originated in Asia Minor. Here the column has its own base, above which a series of bulges and grooves lead to a similarly fluted shaft. The top end of the column, the capital, is rolled up on both sides into the shape of snail-shells. These volutes give the Ionic column its characteristic of ostentation. The Ionic entablature is more lightly and delicately decorated than the Doric.

The last of the three classical orders is the Corinthian. The base, shaft, and also the entablature are similar to the Ionic order, except that the capital is an individual development: it grows out of a garland of leaves that then turn into volutes. This Corinthian variant of the capital, adorned with leaves and buds, re-appeared in Gothic architecture. Before that, however, the columns of the Corinthian order were adopted by Ancient Rome in particular.

above—**CLAUDE PERRAULT, ORDONNANCE FOR THE FIVE KINDS OF COLUMNS AFTER THE METHOD OF THE ANCIENTS** | Paris | 1683.
right—**CARYATIDS AT ERECHTHEUM** | Acropolis.

292 BC—Completion of the Colossus of Rhodes ·· 214 BC—Construction of the Wall of China ····· CLASSICAL ORDERS 20/21

264 BC—Beginning of the First Punic War

c. 225 BC—Destruction of the Colossus of Rhodes

c. 335 BC – 260 BC Sostratus of Cnidus   c. 320 BC – 280 BC Chares of Lindos

"Renaissance architects study the classical orders at extant buildings from the Roman period."

The Romans adopted the classical orders as defined by the Greek architects. In the first century B.C. the Roman author Vitruvius set out their principles in writing in his ten-volume architectural work, *De architectura*. Here he describes Greek temples and establishes the proportions that relate column to entablature in each case. Roman temples demonstrate how the architects of Ancient Rome appropriated the Greek formal language. Unlike Greek architecture, however, the columns built by Roman architects supported arches, not horizontal beams. The Colosseum, which was begun in 72 A.D., shows how the ancient classical orders persisted into the Roman period: from the outside the stories of the amphitheater are not only horizontal, but articulated in axes (fig. left). Arches supported by columns extend around the façade of the building. The three lower stories are built following the traditions of the classical orders most closely. On the ground floor plain Doric capitals top off the shafts of the columns, while, above them, Ionic capitals are used, characterized by their rolled-up corners. On the third story Corinthian capitals created using plant forms are employed. While developments in the different

orders took place even during the Greek period, it was, however, the Romans who were the first to create hybrid forms. They combined the Ionic with the Corinthian variations and thus added another form to the scheme: the Composite order. In the same way, it is only in Roman architecture that we find examples of the Tuscan order: here the shaft of the column is usually left smooth, but in all other respects the column is similar to the Doric variation. With the rediscovery of the cultural riches of Antiquity during the Renaissance, the classical orders too reappeared. Still extant buildings from the Roman period, such as the Colosseum, for example, made the study of the orders possible. At the same time Renaissance architects started to look once again at the writings of Vitruvius. Architectural theorists were the first to pay them any attention. Leon Battista Alberti (1404–72), the embodiment of the Renaissance idea of the universal man not only as a theoretician but also as an architect, sculptor and poet, drew extensively on the architecture of Antiquity. Alberti studied the buildings of Rome and Vitruvius's treatise on architecture, bringing the ideas of art into Antiquity to his own era. In his 1452 work, *De re aedificatoria* [On the Art of Building in Ten Books] he produced his own definition of the three classical orders, which led to a great deal of interest. The architect Donato Bramante (1444–1514) was the

left—THE COLOSSEUM | Rome | AD 72 – 80.

22/23 CLASSICAL ORDERS ········· **196 BC**—Inscription of the Rosetta Stone ··· **146 BC**—Destruction of Carthage ·············

183 BC—Death of Hannibal ·············

first to try to realize his ideas. The Tempietto of S. Pietro in Montorio, Rome, which Bramante built c. 1500 boasted a thorough-going Doric order (fig. right). The round temple is enclosed by a peristyle supporting a balustrade, and the center of the building is surmounted by a dome. In building this little temple Bramante drew on models from Antiquity, thus promoting a concept of architecture which had enormous influence on his contemporaries both within the architectural world and beyond. Bramante himself included the three orders in his numerous sketches for churches in Rome, not the least of which was the interior of St. Peter's Basilica, for which he chose the Corinthian order.

This reversion to Antiquity became the accepted thing, and in the sixteenth century whole hosts of architects applied the classical orders to churches, villas, and palaces. Even *the* villa architect of the sixteenth century, Andrea Palladio (1508–80), frequently referred back to the classical orders in his buildings. Palladio created the entrance to his Villa Rotonda, which he built near Vicenza in 1566, as a temple frontage from Antiquity with six Ionic columns and a triangular pediment. In the second of his *Four Books of Architecture* Palladio explained his use of this element: "In all the buildings for farms and also for some of those in the city I have built a tympanum [*frontespicio*] on the front façade...,

because tympanums accentuate the entrance of the house and contribute greatly to the grandeur and magnificence of the building, thus making the front part more imposing than the others...." (Andrea Palladio, *The Four Books of Architecture*, trans. Robert Tavernor and Richard Schofield, MIT, 1997, p. 147) (see pp. 84–85).

Up until the era of Classicism in the eighteenth and nineteenth centuries the classical orders set the tone of the architectural canon in Europe. The Greek orders appeared once more in the context of city architecture with the Brandenburg Gate. Berlin's last city gate, which has latterly become a symbol of German reunification, was created by Carl Gotthard Langhans (1732–1808) in the late eighteenth century (fig. above). The architect made no secret of his passion for Greece, and in his sketch for the Brandenburg Gate he made reference to the design of the Propylaeum in Athens, the monumental gate on the Acropolis. In the Berlin version six Doric columns support the entablature, as well as the quad-

above—**CARL GOTTHARD LANGHANS, BRANDENBURG GATE** | Berlin 1788 – 91.

right—**DONATO BRAMANTE, TEMPIETTO OF S. PIETRO IN MONTORIO** Rome | *c.* 1500.

100 BC—Birth of Caesar .... **69 BC**—Birth of Cleopatra...

33 BC—Vitruvius begins his treatise *De architectura*...

c. **60 BC – 10 BC Vitruvius**

c. AD 30—Crucifixion of Jesus of Nazareth.. AD 80—Completion of the Colosseum in Rome..... CLASSICAL ORDERS **24/25**

AD 79—Destruction of Pompeii..

"Up until the era of Classicism the classical orders set the tone of the architectural canon in Europe."

riga—Victoria, Roman goddess of victory, in her chariot pulled by four horses. In France too, classical architecture, and with it the classical orders, were very popular. In Paris, for example, Napoleon undertook to complete the unfinished Church of the Madeleine. Now the building was conceived no longer as a church, but as a monument to the French army. Thus the temple form was chosen, which architect Pierre-Alexandre Vignon (1763–1828) carried out beginning in 1807. By the time the project was finished in 1842 the building had been returned to its original purpose, and the Church of the Madeleine became Napoleon's most important contribution to sacred architecture. The exterior is like a temple frontage from Antiquity with a continuous peristyle running around the entire building formed of richly decorated columns in the Corinthian order (fig. left).

left—PIERRE-ALEXANDRE VIGNON, CHURCH OF THE MADELEINE
Paris | 1807–42.

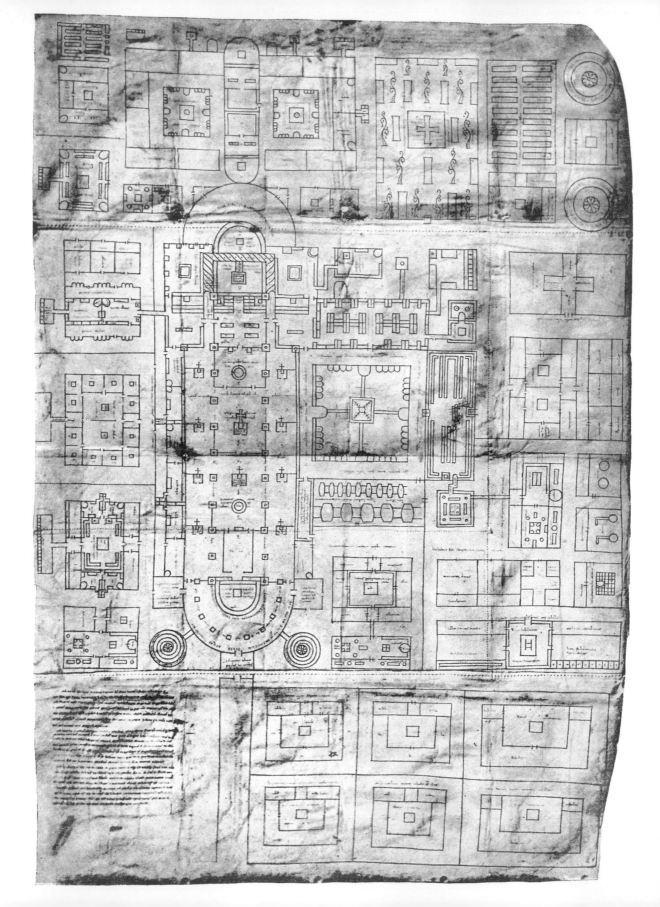

820—Construction of St Michael's Church in Fulda .... 1024—Completion of the Golden Gate in Kiev ....

976—Construction of St Mark's Basilica in Venice ....

1010—First stone laying of St Michael's Church in Hildesheim ....

26/27

THE FIRST ARCHITECTURE ON PAPER

Detailed architectural drawings and computer-aided three-dimensional graphic design have been taken for granted for so long that it is hard to imagine the work of building without them. But until the late Middle Ages it was the exception to commit an imagined building to paper (or parchment) in the form of a sketch or a plan. Blueprints were unheard of. Apart from one single exception no architectural drawings even from the Romanesque period have been found. This makes it all the more astonishing that from the eleventh century onwards building activity increased markedly. Plans themselves, however, were probably not used in big building projects such as churches or monasteries. Instead the architect would mark out the ground-plan immediately and took all other measurements directly during the building process, as soon as the proportions of the different parts of the building were established. Thus in the first instance a building project only existed in the architect's imagination.

As a result, the oldest surviving architectural drawing from the Middle Ages, the Plan of St. Gall in Switzerland, has great rarity value (fig. left). But here it is more a question of a representation of an architectural ideal than of an actual building plan. The Plan of St. Gall was drawn up *c.* 830 in an abbey on the island of Reichenau on Lake Constance in Germany, and was sent to the abbot of the Abbey of St. Gall, who was planning a new church. Numerous components of an abbey structure are drawn in red ink on parchment, and the functions of the individual buildings are marked. At the center there is a basilica with three naves, and connected on the right-hand side there is a cloister as well as monks' cells, and around these are grouped the workshops. To the left of the church there is the abbot's house and a visitors' house, and at the top of the page there is the doctor's house, a hospital with cloisters, and the cloister garden. Even if this is not a real architectural drawing but an idealized concept of an abbey as a city in miniature, the Plan of St. Gall is remarkable. In the end architectural drawings only came into use during the late Gothic period, so this ninth-century drawing stands alone, an isolated example.

At the beginning of the thirteenth century, medieval building activity changed. With the development of city life, building projects extended into the secular world: no longer was it a question of building churches and monasteries, but also town halls, guildhalls, hospitals, and merchants' houses. The workshops of the monasteries were gradually separated from those

left—**PLAN OF ST. GALL** | *c.* 830 | Abbey Library of St. Gall.

1096—Beginning of the First Crusade .... **1271**—First sea voyage of Marco Polo.................

c. 1115—Construction of Angkor Wat.................

1377 – 1446 Filippo Brunelleschi

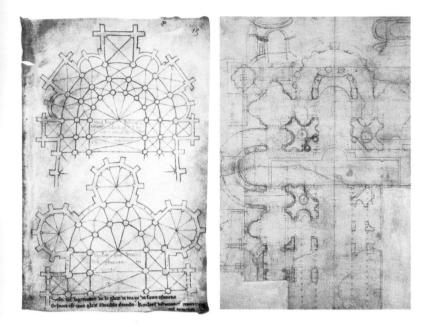

of the town. These new forms of organization go hand-in-hand with the appearance of architectural drawing to scale. Plans and elevations, joinery plans, and templates now formed the basis of the building process. Plans simplified processes in the architectural workshops: they show a section through a building and illustrate the foundation walls and supports, but they also sum up the structure of the vaulting. Such drawings were tools in architectural planning; architects no longer had to rely exclusively on practical experience. They also provided advantages for the architects, as through the drawings and plans the costs entailed in a new building could be calculated. The French architect Villard de Honnecourt collected numerous plans and elevations in his architectural sketchbook. The work, compiled c. 1230, is the most important source on the subject of building activity in the High Middle Ages. Through the drawings Honnecourt showed mainly existing buildings, including the numerous cathedrals of his time, but he also found new solutions based on his structural records. Thus for Vaucelles Abbey in northern France he drew the plan of the choir of the church and then sketched a new choir, placing square chapels between the round ones and designing a second ambulatory (fig. above left).

The ever-increasing number of drawings of plans, created from the late Middle Ages onwards, had not only a practical significance for the execution of a building. Rather, in the architects' workshop they were also afforded high status as models and given to apprentices to copy. Architectural drawings also offered the possibility, in light of the frequently long hiatuses in building and changes in architect, of maintaining continuity. The monumental west façade of Cologne Cathedral, for example, was already determined to a large extent when its foundation stone was laid in 1248. However, it was only built in the nineteenth century when a renewed interest in medieval architecture ensured that buildings begun many centuries before were completed. In the case of Cologne Cathedral this was possible thanks to the enormous plan that was preserved of the façade. The so-called *Plan F* was created c. 1300 and shows on twenty sheets of parchment four meters long every detail of the west façade (fig. right).

As in the Middle Ages, so in the Renaissance too the floor layout of a building was the most important means of planning. For the rebuilding of St. Peter's Basilica in Rome, which was to grow into one of the largest building sites of its time, a ground-plan on squared paper was prepared. This grid helped to check the proportions of the building. The drawing, to which architect Donato Bramante contributed, shows several planning stages one on top of another. Starting on the left-hand side the current situation of

1444–1514 Donato Bramante   1475–1564 Michelangelo Buonarroti

"Architectural drawings offered the possibility, in light of the frequently long hiatuses in building and changes in architect, of maintaining continuity."

St. Peter's in 1505/06 is established; however, at the top of the sheet two perspective drawings can be seen. In the large architectural workshops of St. Peter's advances were also made in the way architecture was represented in the sixteenth century: ground-plan, elevation, section, and different perspective views of a building were shown alongside each other, in order to ensure the most comprehensive and therefore unambiguous graphic representation possible. While such exact building plans showing several perspective views of a building became the norm by the end of the fifteenth century, it would be a good four hundred years yet before uniform standards for architectural plans were implemented.

far left—VAUCELLES ABBEY, THE PORTFOLIO OF VILLARD DE HONNE-
COURT | *c.* 1230.
left—ST. PETER'S | Rome | 1505/06 | 20A recto | Uffizi Galleries, Florence.
right—COLOGNE CATHEDRAL, PLAN F | *c.* 1300.

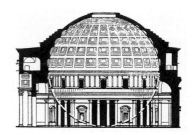

THE FIRST DOMES

Architects discovered thousands of years ago that they could enclose spaces not only with a flat ceiling, but also by using a semi-circular vault. This curved ceiling was suitable above all for centrally planned buildings, that is buildings which were planned on a round or square footprint. Domes were frequently used in Antiquity, and in Byzantine architecture they were part of a permanent formal vocabulary, being used primarily in mosques. At the end of the Middle Ages the vaulted form of the dome also experienced a renaissance, as demonstrated by the brilliant achievement of the dome of Florence Cathedral. However dome building had already reached its first peak 1,300 years earlier, in the Pantheon in Rome. This temple dedicated to all the gods (in Latin *pantheum* means "to every god") is among the best preserved monuments of ancient Rome. The circular structure was built between 118 and 125 A.D. and remained in use as a Christian church even after the Roman period. A wide portico stands in front of the circular temple building and leads to the domed interior (fig. above). The dome is as high as it is wide, and as the section shows, it was designed in the shape of a perfect sphere. The diameter of the rotunda is 43 meters, and this is the same as the height of the walls from the floor to the vertex of the dome. Light enters the interior through a round, nine-meter-wide opening in the center of the vault: this topmost oculus is the only source of light in the Pantheon. The dome is decorated on the inside with coffering: the five rows of sunken square panels reduce in size towards the oculus and intensify the effect of great height. The material of which the dome is made is a kind of lightweight concrete, to which a mortar of volcanic stones was added in order to reduce the net weight. The Pantheon in Rome is not only the largest dome in the ancient world but is also the largest dome to be created by being molded as a single unit.

Domes were of great importance in Byzantine architecture, as demonstrated by the Hagia Sophia, which was built in Constantinople (now Istanbul) between 532 and 537 (fig. p. 33). The capital of the Byzantine Empire was an important cultural and trade center in the early Middle Ages and the new Church of Holy Wisdom lived up to this status: for centuries the Hagia Sophia was by far the greatest church in Christendom. The ground-plan of the building is a unique invention, as in the Hagia Sophia it unites the longitudinally planned basilica with the centrally planned building. As such the church has

left—**Pantheon** | Rome | AD 118 – 125 | interior view of the cupola.
right—**Pantheon** | Rome | AD 118 – 125 | elevation.

442–537 Isidore of Miletus   2nd half of the 5th C. – before 558 Anthemius of Tralles

an imposing vaulted roof, and an unsupported dome dominates the main space. The dome is almost 56 meters high and has a diameter of 31 meters. Further smaller domes complete the west and east sides of the building.

The architects Anthemius of Tralles and Isidore of Miletus created a technical masterpiece in the construction of this dome. The main dome is supported by pendentives, whereby an imaginary circle slices horizontally across the arches of the church and then a hemisphere is placed on this surface. The triangles which arise from the transition from square ground-plan to the circular form of the dome are known as pendentives. The ingenious dome construction of the Hagia Sophia collapsed, albeit only in part, as a result of an earthquake just a year after its inauguration. The impact on the dome had apparently shifted the pillars and load-bearing arches outwards. Reconstruction began immediately, and the new dome, now six meters higher, was already finished by 562. After the conquest of Constantinople by Sultan Mehmet II the Hagia Sophia, which had been both cathedral and the church of court and state, was converted into the most important mosque of the Ottoman Empire. This function is indicated by the four minarets, which still characterize the external appearance of the building. It is now used as a museum.

In the Middle Ages longitudinally planned buildings became more important than centrally planned ones, and so domes lagged behind by comparison with the groin-vaulted choirs, naves, and aisles of the great churches. During the Renaissance, however, centrally planned buildings were considered the epitome of symmetry and harmony and so monumental domes once again attracted the interest of architects. In this respect, the city of Florence and architect Filippo Brunelleschi (1377–1446) opened up a rich line of development (fig. p. 34).

Building work on the cathedral of Santa Maria del Fiore in the center of Florence had been in progress since 1296, but the vaulting of the dome still had to be completed. The gigantic extent of the plan had already been sketched out: an eight-sided, fenestrated drum; the wall supporting the dome was over 41 meters in diameter and no less than 50 meters high. This cathedral dome was intended to outstrip that brilliant achievement of the ancient world, the dome of the Pantheon. Filippo Brunelleschi, who had

above—GIOVANNI PAOLO PANINI, THE INTERIOR OF THE PANTHEON, ROME | *c.* 1740 | oil on canvas | 128 × 99 cm.

right—HAGIA SOPHIA | Istanbul | 532 – 537.

.... **1010**—First stone laying of St Michael's Church in Hildesheim .... **1271**—First sea voyage of Marco Polo···· **DOMES** 34/35

1096—Beginning of the First Crusade ....

***c.* 1115**—Construction of Angkor Wat ....

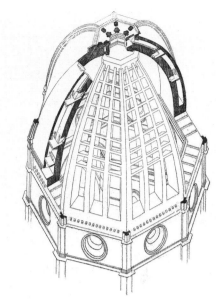

won the competition to finish the dome, took on the task, beginning his spectacular feat of engineering in 1420. His solution for the future symbol of Florence was a double-shelled dome by means of which he achieved a new dimension in the art of vaulting (fig. above). Together the inner shell, which is over two meters thick, and the thinner outer shell, along with the ribs which link them together, absorb the forces created by the dome. To let in light, the unsupported dome, like its Roman predecessor, is open at its vertex. Brunelleschi added a finishing touch to this oculus in the dome, the lantern. Constructing a vault over a building of this size presented the architect with a technical problem as well. It was not possible to erect supporting scaffolding from the floor of the church because of the building's great height; and working with a cradle was too unsafe because of the huge diameter of the space. Brunelleschi also ventured into uncharted territory technically, designing a system by which the dome could be vaulted while supporting itself at the same time.

The dome of Florence Cathedral heralded the beginning of a long analysis of the buildings of the ancient world, above all the Pantheon. The building of St. Peter's Basilica in Rome, for example, was another attempt to outdo the Pantheon and thus can be seen as emulating the dome of the cathedral in Florence. Michelangelo began building the immense dome in the middle of the sixteenth century. In the event, he was unable to surpass the Pantheon dome in terms of its span, but succeeded in outdoing the ancient model by achieving a height of 136 meters (fig. p. 37). Michaelangelo's dome for St. Peter's was a point of reference until well into the Baroque period, in particular in its impact from a distance: the dome which is visible from the outside is considerably higher than the dome built over the interior space. Domes appear in the most varied types of vault construction, and not only in Renaissance and Baroque churches. They also featured in residential buildings: Andrea Palladio (1508–80), the most sought-after villa architect of the Renaissance, also drew on the ancient temple form and introduced the dome into his designs for villas in the Veneto (see also pp. 84/85). Numerous palaces were adorned with domed rooms; and in the eighteenth and nineteenth centuries even government buildings acquired domes, for example the United States Capitol in Washington.

left—Filippo Brunelleschi, Cathedral of Santa Maria del Fiore | Florence | dome from 1420.

above—Florence Cathedral, section.

1347—Outbreak of the plague in Europe
c. 1455—Gutenberg invents the printing press
1517—Beginning of Reformation (Martin Luther's *95 Theses*)

1377–1446 Filippo Brunelleschi   1404–1472 Leon Battista Alberti   1475–1564 Michelangelo Buonarroti   1598–1680 Gian Lorenzo Bernini

1618—Beginning of the Thirty Years' War .... **1939–1945**—Second World War··· **DOMES** 36/37

1914–1918—First World War ································

1776—Declaration of Independence in the USA ·········

1662–1736 Matthäus Daniel Pöppelmann .... 1870–1947 Max Berg

In the twentieth century, the invention of reinforced concrete introduced completely new possibilities for domed architecture as well. The range of concrete forms that were now available to architects was illustrated by Max Berg (1870–1947), for example, in his spectacular design for The Centennial Hall in Wrocław, Poland (formerly known in German as Breslau), which the architect topped with a dome (fig. left). The large interior space of the Hall, which was completed in 1913 and was built to commemorate the uprising against Napoleon, consists of a vault 65 meters wide formed of reinforced concrete ribs. The 35 ribs come together like a star to form a ring, which is in turn surmounted by a small cupola. Around the four rings, which are stacked one on top of the other to create the dome, are continuous windows. Thus the construction of the dome remains visible, as broad, round arches form a continuation of the ribs and direct the structural forces into the foundations of the building.

left—MAX BERG, THE CENTENNIAL HALL | Wrocław (Breslau), Poland
1911–13 | view of interior of dome.
above—MICHELANGELO, ST. PETER'S BASILICA | Rome | dome 1547–90.
next double page spread—FRANK LLOYD WRIGHT, SOLOMON R. GUGGEN-
HEIM MUSEUM | 1943–59 | view of the cupola.

476—End of the Western Roman Empire ············ **c. 570**—Birth of the Prophet Muhammad ························
·······**532**—Construction of Hagia Sophia ··
40/41

442–537 Isidore of Miletus   **2nd half of the 5th C. – before 558 Anthemius of Tralles**

HOW THE BASILICA BECAME A CHURCH

In the Middle Ages the most important architectural task was church building. Whether parish churches or monasteries, simple churches for mendicant orders or magnificent cathedrals, the requirements for sacred buildings created innumerable large building projects all over Europe. With the basilica form church building imposed a building type that had originally fulfilled quite different purposes. The basilica is not a medieval invention—they had already been developed in ancient Rome and frequently built there. In the Roman era basilicas served as assembly halls for all kinds of uses. They were law courts, places of worship, and even market halls. When Emperor Constantine acknowledged Christianity at the beginning of the fourth century, a lot of new church building began. The Emperor himself, or his bishops, founded churches, and soon the basilica was established as the building form for this task. Santa Sabina in Rome is a basilica from the early Christian period (fig. pp. 46/47). The church was built c. 430 A.D. on the Aventine Hill, on the site where the house of the martyr St. Sabina is thought to have stood. A glimpse of the interior shows the orientation of the church: the longitudinal axis ends

with a semi-circular space called the apse, and the building is orientated towards this. The nave has a flat ceiling, and the upper section of the walls is set with round-headed windows. Below, round arches create the entrance to the side aisles. This sums up the characteristics of a basilica: it consists of a high central aisle illuminated independently by windows, and lower side aisles, which are separated from the central section by arches. The easterly end of the church is formed by the semi-circular apse, which contains the altar.

In medieval Christian teaching, each architectural component of a basilica had a particular meaning. This started with the orientation of the buildings: basilicas face eastwards as, according to Christian belief, this means they point in the direction of the Holy Land. The clear orientation of these elongated buildings contrasts with centrally planned buildings, which are based on a symmetrical ground-plan, taking the form of a circle or an octagon, for example. According to the orientation of a basilica the entrance faces west, while the choir is located in the east of the church. The west façade with the main entrance was understood to be the entrance to the house of God and was accentuated with towers or a porch.

In the Romanesque period the basilica was finally established as the building form for churches. Yet the

left—SPEYER CATHEDRAL, VIEW FROM THE WEST | 1025–61.

"Building a basilica was oriented on Christian belief: basilicas face eastwards in the direction of the Holy Land."

concept of Romanesque is a 19th-century invention. It is understood to mean art from the eleventh to the mid-thirteenth centuries, a period when architecture reverted to forms from Roman Antiquity. In fact it was only after the turn of the millennium that clear correspondences in artistic production emerged in France, Spain, Italy, Germany, and England, despite regional differences. It is an aspect of this international common ground in Romanesque architecture that the basilica is the most frequently used type of sacred building. Another characteristic of the architecture of this period is the round arch. The construction of arches, which had already been employed in Roman architecture, was taken up again by the architects of the Romanesque period. In church interiors there were to be no more straight-headed openings, but instead round arches supported by columns and pillars. The construction of stone roofs was also tackled using round arches. The vaulting, firstly of the side aisles, then of the church's central aisle as well, is a further characteristic of the Romanesque style. Sculptural elements attached to the architecture were also used more and more at this time: the portals and façades of Romanesque buildings were shaped in a rich sculptural and ornamental way. An excellent example of this is the Pórtico de la Gloria on the west façade of the great pilgrimage church of Santiago de Compostela in Spain, which has been the main entrance to the basilica since the late twelfth century (fig. p. 44). One of the first buildings that shows the essential features of Romanesque architecture is the cathedral in Speyer, Germany, which was begun in the years after 1020 (fig. p. 40). The plan of the church shows the basilica form. In addition, between the nave and the choir a section of the building has been introduced at right angles: this is the transept, a typical feature of Romanesque sacred architecture. Thus the ground-plan of the body of the church forms a cross. The cathedral in Speyer was planned as the burial place for the Salian emperors: Conrad II, who ascended the throne as first Salian emperor in 1027, ordered work to begin on his church around 1030. The entrance lies within a massive westwork (west-facing entrance section), its central axis surmounted by a tower. Beyond this is a three-aisled nave. The transept intersects with the nave in front of the east-facing, semi-circular choir. This point, at which the spatial axes of nave and transept meet, the so-called crossing, is marked on the outside of the building by a tower. Two further towers are attached to the choir area, which can be recognized on the plan as

right—SAINT-LAZARE | Autun | 1120 – 46 | north wall of the nave.

········ **1010**—First stone laying of St Michael's Church in Hildesheim ·· **1271**—First sea voyage of Marco Polo··· **BASILICA** 44/45

·· **1096**—Beginning of the First Crusade ··

·· **c. 1115**—Construction of Angkor Wat ··

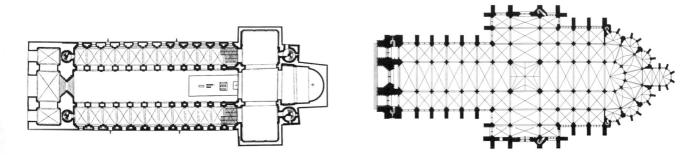

a semi-circle. Like many Romanesque church build-ings, Speyer Cathedral seen from the outside looks as if it has been made up of individual architectural elements joined together. This would change with the advent of the Gothic cathedrals. Even in the late Middle Ages, however, the ground-plan of the basilica remained dominant. This was the case too for Amiens Cathedral, which was begun in the period of High Gothic, around 200 years after Speyer (fig. above left). In its ground-plan it is above all the east-facing part of the church which is emphasized by comparison

with Romanesque buildings: already the transept has three aisles, attached to which are even more vaulted areas of the nave, which in its transition to the choir, has five aisles. For a long time now the choir area has no longer been just a semi-circular apse: instead, at-tached to this is an ambulatory, which is surrounded by more semi-circular apses. Even if the shape of the choir in particular in Gothic cathedrals was essenti-ally more extravagant than in Romanesque churches, the basic form of the basilica remained the most influ-ential in Western church architecture for centuries.

left—CATHEDRAL OF SANTIAGO DE COMPOSTELA, PÓRTICO DE LA GLORIA ON THE WEST FAÇADE | late 12th century.

above left—SPEYER CATHEDRAL, GROUND-PLAN OF THE BUILDING 1025–61.

above right—AMIENS CATHEDRAL, GROUND-PLAN OF THE NAVE from 1220.

next double page spread—SANTA SABINA | Rome | 425–c. 432.

VAULTED CEILINGS

In Greek temples horizontal stone beams were supported by tall columns, as exemplified by the famous Parthenon built in the fifth century B.C. on the Acropolis in Athens (see p. 16 and 17). With the arrival of Roman architecture the curved arch won its place alongside the straight beam. For functional buildings such as aqueducts, pillars supporting arches were used equally, as in the building of the Roman Colosseum (see fig. p. 20). And alongside the development of the arch in the Roman period we see that of the curved, self-supporting stone ceiling which covers a space—the vault.

The different variations on the vault, whose common basic form is the arc, permit a wealth of spatial solutions, from architecturally simple barrel-vaulted spaces via dome constructions to Gothic variations using stellar vaulting and fan vaulting. The dome flourished during the period of Byzantine architecture. One of the most important domed churches is the Hagia Sophia in Istanbul (see also The First Domes, pp. 30–33).

It was above all the Romans who developed the use of vaulting in architecture. But knowledge of how to create vaults across spaces was not used in the first instance in temple building—where they preferred to stick to Greek models—but in the architecture of Roman baths. Every town in the Roman Empire had its own public baths, which were an important part of social life. The lofty halls of the baths were vaulted, as shown for example in the reconstruction of the huge site of the Baths of Caracalla from the early 3rd century A.D. While the central bathing rooms were vaulted with a hemispherical dome, the elongated rooms were barrel-vaulted, with many arcs placed alongside each other. If two barrel-vaulted rooms of equal height came together, this created a groin vault. The Romans developed the groin vault out of the barrel vault and used it to cover wide spaces. The vault was used even for places of religious worship such as temples and early Christian basilicas, particularly from late Antiquity onwards.

The Pantheon in Rome, a temple dedicated to all the gods, with its dome of over 43 meters in diameter, occupies a special place in the dome architecture of ancient Rome.

At first the groin vault maintained its position of great importance in medieval architecture. In church building after the turn of the millennium a plan with three aisles was the norm, with two side aisles flanking a wider, higher central aisle. In Romanesque churches, or basilicas, as these three-aisled buildings

left—**Durham Cathedral** | before 1133.

are called, the narrower side aisles were the first to be vaulted, while the central aisle retained its flat ceiling. The use of vaulting in church aisles is one of the great innovations of Romanesque architecture. Where groin vaulting was introduced in Romanesque architecture, the space to be covered was at the outset still very small. The architects began with small spaces and gradually vaulted the entire space of the church.

In Speyer Cathedral the vaulting of the individual architectural sections similarly took place in several stages (fig. above). The cathedral, the burial place of the Salian emperors and kings, is the greatest early Romanesque building in the Western world. The monumental three-aisled basilica was rebuilt and extended many times, and in this process it was gradually filled with vaulting. Around the middle of the eleventh century the groin vaults in the underground burial chapel, the crypt, as well as those in the towers and side aisles of the nave were completed. Because of its ridges, the intersecting lines of the surfaces of the vaults which arise due to the fusion of two barrel vaults, this kind of vaulting is also known as cross vaulting. The ridges, which run diagonally, divide the vault into four sections that ensure an equal distribution of the forces created by the vault. In spite of the well-developed technology, several decades passed before the vaulting of the

large expanse of the nave was attempted at Speyer Cathedral. The nave was initially flat-ceilinged and was only later covered with groin vaulting in the years around 1100.

The first time vaulting was used extensively was in the building of Durham Cathedral in England. This three-aisled basilica was begun in 1093, and was completed a good three decades later. This enormous church, 143 meters long, is characterized by strong walls and massive round arches. The architectural forms and technology of cathedral building were brought to England by the Norman conquerors, when William, duke of Normandy, occupied the country in 1066. As a result Norman building styles spread into areas north of the English Channel.

In 1100 the choir of the church saw the introduction of a high vault, which offered a clear contrast to the massive forms of the Romanesque style. The nave vault was finally introduced instead of the originally planned flat ceiling. By 1133 vaulting had been

above—CRYPT OF SPEYER CATHEDRAL | 1025–61.

right—VLADISLAV HALL, HRADČANY (CASTLE DISTRICT) | Prague.

976—Construction of St Mark's Basilica in Venice ················· c. 1115—Construction of Angkor Wat··· VAULTED CEILINGS 52/53
1010—First stone laying of St Michael's Church in Hildesheim···············
1096—Beginning of the First Crusade························

"The idea of vaulted ceilings was first developed in Roman baths architecture and was used in temple building afterwards."

perfected, with the addition of a new type of vault. Thin ridges divide the areas of the vaulting into four sections and below these edges thin ribs are inserted—unlike the crypt of Speyer Cathedral. In this rib vault the rod-like ribs bear the thrust and the cells are stretched between them. In Durham Cathedral the thrust of the vault is diverted by powerful round pillars whose diameter measures as much as six meters. They are decorated with different patterns, including the zigzag form typical of Norman art.

The rib vault soon developed into the standard type of vaulting for the great Gothic cathedrals. By supporting the vaults by means of buttresses and flying buttresses, architects were able to attain spectacular heights with their vaults. The Gothic rib vault was best suited to cover all types of spaces. Its use of pointed arches gave the architect more creative freedom as he could vary the width and height of the vault's sections. The church of Saint-Denis in Paris is one of the first to be built using rib vaulting in the choir. Its high interior was completely vaulted as early as the first quarter of the twelfth century (see fig. p. 58). In the cathedral of Notre-Dame on the Île

de la Cité in Paris, which was begun just a short time later, the vaulting already shows the Gothic form of reaching to the heavens. The church is 130 meters long; its two aisles flank the nave whose vault is an already impressive 35 meters high. The sexpartite vault of the nave of Notre-Dame was completed in c. 1200 (fig. p. 54 above left).

In the late Gothic period rib vaulting developed into ever-more imaginative variations. In the different artistic landscapes regional phenomena emerged in which the rib, originally important to the construction, increasingly became a decorative element, and ultimately covered the surface of the vault as an entire network of ribs. Decorative types of rib in stellar, net and fan vaulting evolved in England and Germany in particular. The development of a vault structure divided into small sections can be seen in the Lady Chapel of Gloucester Cathedral, for example. This apsidal chapel was completed around 1500 and displays a richly decorated vault—a network of ribs with stone bosses set at their intersecting points (fig. p. 54 above right).

The Renaissance saw a return to barrel vaulting in church architecture. In addition this period brought a new flourishing of dome building, beginning with the construction of the dome in Florence (see The First Domes, pp. 30–39).

left—HANS VON BURGHAUSEN, CHURCH OF THE HOLY SPIRIT
Landshut | 1407–61.

above left—**Notre-Dame Cathedral** | Paris | begun 1163.
above right—**Lady Chapel, Gloucester Cathedral** | *c.* 1500.
right—**Gloucester Cathedral, Cloister** | 2nd half of the 14th century.
next double page spread—**Notre-Dame de Senlis** | 1153–91, vault of the nave.

BRIGHTER, HIGHER, FURTHER: THE FIRST CATHEDRALS

The twelfth century saw the growth of towns, which developed into cultural centers. Firstly this led to the development of new building requirements: for example town halls were now necessary, and hospitals and schools were built. And secondly massive churches were also created in the towns of the late Middle Ages. Many of them were only completed centuries after building work began, as the Gothic cathedrals were conceived on a huge scale. Here architects developed Romanesque forms further and adapted them to the requirements of each plan. The transition between periods was fluid during this time. Gradually a new architectural language emerged, which became dominant from around the middle of the twelfth century. The development of Gothic forms began in the French crown land of Île-de-France, but the new architectural style soon spread throughout the whole of Europe.

The Basilica of Saint-Denis in Paris, burial place of the French kings, is one of the founding buildings of the Gothic style. The former abbey church was partially rebuilt in the twelfth century. In the process the choir was enlarged to create more space for the many pilgrims who arrived to worship its relics.

A glimpse into Saint-Denis' extended choir, which was built between 1140 and 1144, demonstrates the architectural achievements of the period (fig. left). The Gothic cathedrals, like the Romanesque churches before them, followed the basilica layout, but now the side aisles led to an ambulatory. Even the choir of Saint-Denis has such a corridor, from which a whole crescent of individual chapels radiates. In this part of the building the pointed arches are immediately noticeable, as they were used both for the arched entrances to the chapels, and also in the windows. The pointed arch allowed considerably more creative freedom than the round arch: according to the demands of each space the pointed arch could be built in a flatter or more upright shape. A new form of vault derived from the pointed arch also emerged, the rib vault, as now spaces of different heights could contain arches of equal height. Rib vaulting can be seen in the choir of Saint-Denis: its bulging ribs divide the individual vault sections and merge into the pillars (see Vaulted Ceilings, pp. 48–57). Only these columns and diaphragm arches separate the ambulatory from the crescent of chapels, and there are no dividing walls between the chapels themselves. The overall impression is of an open interior space, illuminated by areas of fenestration.

Pointed arches and rib vaulting are fundamental characteristics of Gothic architecture, and their

left—CHOIR OF THE BASILICA OF SAINT-DENIS | 1140 – 44.

60/61 CATHEDRALS .... **1157**—Birth of Richard I of England .... **1173**—First known influenza epidemic ....

.... **1173**—First stone laying of the Tower of Pisa

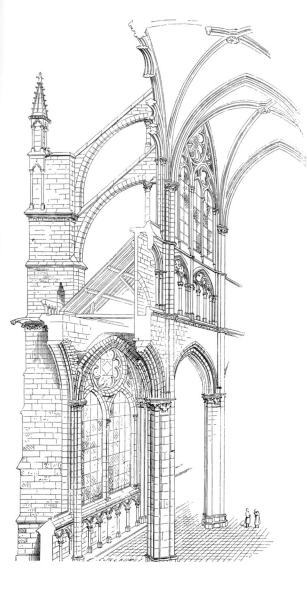

creative advantages were fully exploited during this period. Because of the lighter weight of rib vaulting, Gothic architects could use it to cover larger areas than the previously used barrel or cross vaulting. In rib vaulting slender columns bear the load. However, the thrust of the vault is not only downwards into the columns, but also sideways.

In order to absorb this sideways thrust, Gothic architects developed the system of buttresses, a central element of construction in the great cathedrals. To this end, arches were attached to the outside of the nave, above the height of the side aisles (fig. left). These flying buttresses are supported by masonry piers, which are built outside against the side aisle at right-angles to the church wall. The piers form a structural unit with the so-called engaged columns inside the church, the slender columns which support the ribs. As a result both flying buttresses and vaulting must be built at the same time, so that no one-sided loads are brought to bear on the walls

left—**NAVE OF AMIENS CATHEDRAL** | 1220 – 36 | section.
right—**VIEW OF THE CHOIR OF AMIENS CATHEDRAL**.
next double page spread—**LAON CATHEDRAL** | 1170 – 1235
view of the nave.

of the nave. The piers and flying buttresses on the outside of the church are often decorated, as is the case in Amiens Cathedral (see p. 61). And as Amiens Cathedral also demonstrates, flying buttresses can also be double. As naves increase in height two or even three flying buttresses one above the other are necessary to absorb the thrust of the vault. Buttressing was not only attached to the nave, but it also absorbed the thrust of the vaulting in the choir area. Over time the initially heavy and deep flying buttresses became thinner and thinner, as can be seen for example in the buttressing of the choir at Chartres Cathedral, which was built between 1210 and 1220. In this small town southwest of Paris, building on a large church began in 1194 after its predecessor had been destroyed by fire (fig. above left). The west façade of Chartres Cathedral is surmounted by two spires of different heights, which mark the parameters of the building's architectural history: the lower south spire dates from an earlier period of building, while the north spire, completed in 1506, displays the rich ornamentation of the Gothic period. The nave and transept were built in just 25 years: by 1220 the church was complete, apart from individual sections such as the north spire mentioned above. In light of the church's overall length of 130 meters, this short building schedule is all the more astonishing.

In these few years, buttressing developed into a decorative element: piers and flying buttresses abutting the nave and choir are ornamented with small towers on the piers, and curved arcades are set into the lower part of the buttress (fig. above right). Thus buttresses did not remain a purely functional form for long, but soon became a creative element that determined the visual impact of Gothic cathedrals in a fundamental way. Alongside architectural sculpture and ornamentation, which were an equally important and multiform component of Gothic churches, buttresses in their numerous variations made the external architecture less severe. The massiveness of Romanesque churches, and the impression they gave of having been assembled from different architectural elements, has been left far behind. Thanks to the innovations of Gothic architecture, churches shot skywards: the nave of Chartres, for example, boasts an impressive interior height of 37 meters.

above left—CHARTRES CATHEDRAL | view from the north.
above right—BUTTRESSING ON THE CHOIR OF CHARTRES CATHEDRAL before 1220.
right—INTERIOR OF THE SAINTE-CHAPELLE | Paris | 1241 – 48.

1210—Founding of the Franciscan Order ··· CATHEDRALS **66/67**

····························· **1215**—Founding of the Dominican Order ···

"The Gothic cathedrals were conceived on a huge scale – many of them were only completed centuries after building work began."

It is precisely in the system of buttressing that the polished technical construction of Gothic cathedrals can be clearly discerned (fig. p. 64), construction which the architects undertook without the aid of structural calculations. This construction relied exclusively on general ideas about how structural forces operated. Particularly in light of the great heights which were being built it is scarcely credible that medieval architects could manage without exact knowledge of the effect of dead weight or wind load on the structure. But in fact medieval building plans were based on experiential values as they affected the load-bearing capacity of materials and constructions. Statics, which would be used to make exact calculations possible, only appeared in the eighteenth century. As a result, building collapses and repairs were an everyday occurrence: for example, the entire vaulting of Beauvais Cathedral, whose nave was said to have reached the remarkable height of 48 meters, collapsed in 1284. And the sixteenth century saw the collapse of the crossing tower during the ongoing rebuilding of the church. Nevertheless the striving for height in Gothic cathedral building still did not cease. Interiors as well as exteriors with towers on their façades and crossings all emphasized increasingly the upward movement.

In Gothic cathedrals the walls had largely handed over their load-bearing function to the buttresses. The architects knew how to exploit this structural development: large wall surfaces disappeared and light was declared to be the new center of attention in churches. In place of massive masonry, architectural frameworks appeared which incorporated progressively larger window openings, creating interiors flooded with light. This is particularly noticeable in the Sainte-Chapelle in Paris. King Louis IX commissioned the building of the chapel in the mid-thirteenth century next to his palace on the Île de la Cité. The over 12-meter-high windows were divided by stone partitions between whose thin, masonry tracery the colored glass pieces were set. Thus entire glass tapestries composed of colorful, radiant windows form the walls of the church. Light falls through the glass onto the delicate, richly decorated and painted architecture of the interior (fig. p. 65).

Beyond France too, Gothic architectural forms became dominant in many places, and with them the idea of space filled with colored light as the epitome of Gothic architecture. In the twelfth and thirteenth centuries cathedrals were built in England, Spain, and Germany on the model of the French churches.

left—LINCOLN CATHEDRAL, ANGEL CHOIR | 1256–1320.

In Cologne, for example, work began in 1248 on a massive building which adopted Gothic architectural forms. The height of the space also increased: the nave of Cologne Cathedral reached over 43 meters in height. Thus a new standard was set in the development of height, and certainly in the question of building schedule as well: Cologne Cathedral was only finally finished in the nineteenth century after a long hiatus in building activity. At this time the Gothic style, and with it the entire Middle Ages, were undergoing a renaissance: country villas and garden features appeared in the neo-Gothic style, and at the same time the Gothic cathedrals were subjected to expert investigation and restoration. In the Romantic period in particular the enthusiasm for the Middle Ages reached its peak in Germany, supported by Johann Wolfgang von Goethe. The poet recorded his admiration for the Gothic Strasbourg Cathedral in an essay of 1773: Gothic architecture was now the only true form (fig. right). The young Goethe enthusiastically praised "the builder who heaped up mountains into the clouds." (*Goethe's Literary Essays*, ed. J.E. Spingarn, New York 1921)

above—**Jean Fouquet, Building a Gothic Cathedral**
Antiquities and Wars of the Jews | illuminated manuscript end of the 15th century.
right—**West façade of Strasbourg Cathedral.**

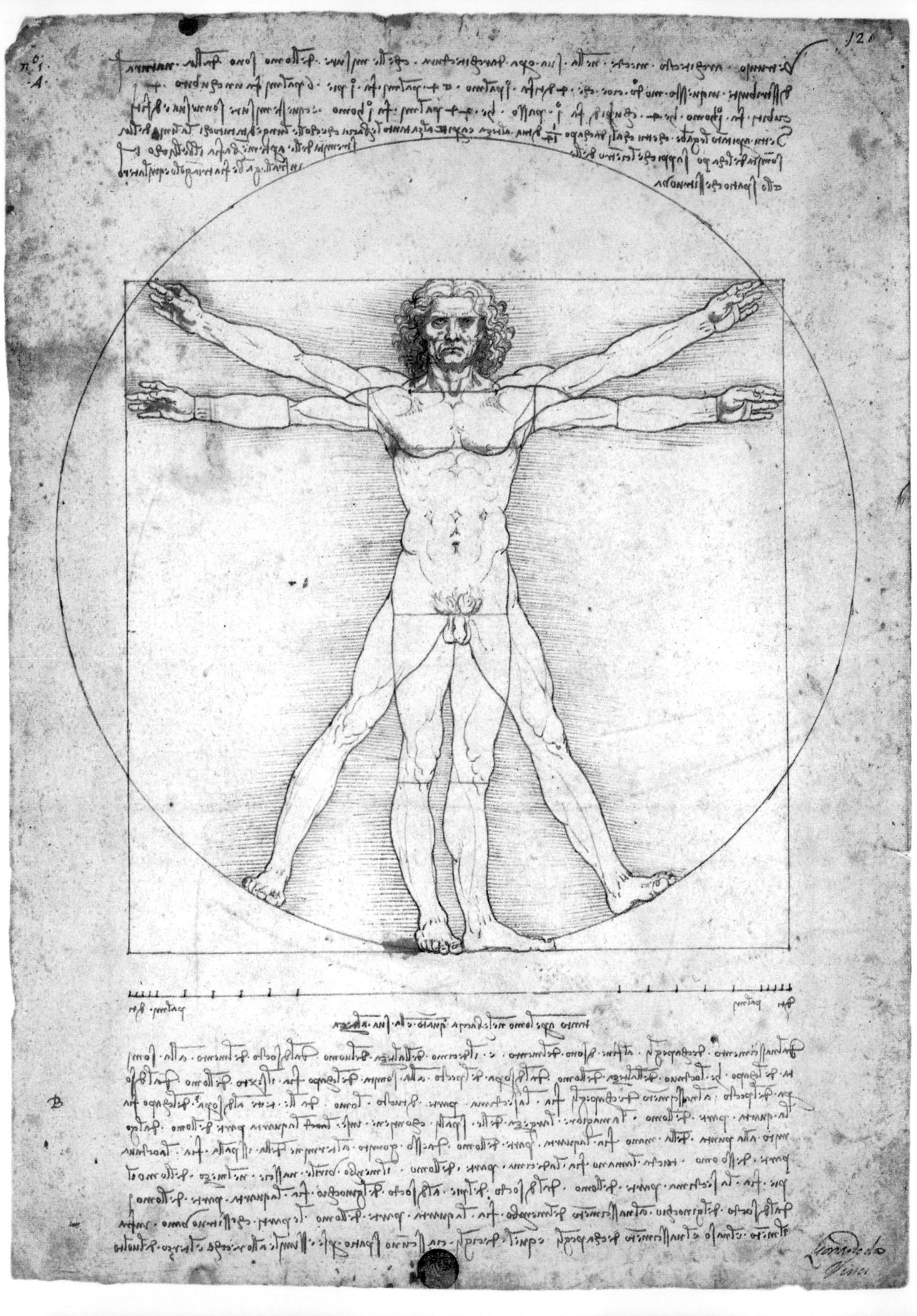

1377–1446 Filippo Brunelleschi

MAN BECOMES THE MEASURE OF ALL THINGS: RENAISSANCE ARCHITECTURE

During the fifteenth and sixteenth centuries, the wide-ranging revivals of the Renaissance prepared the way for the modern age. The concept of renaissance expresses the idea of a re-birth, and the entire period was characterized by a cultural reorientation towards Antiquity. The literature of Antiquity was to be opened up as comprehensively as possible and made accessible again; classical Latin was rediscovered and taught; even ancient Greece became a subject of study once more. The dissemination of knowledge was made all the more possible by the introduction of the printed book. Books took the place of manuscripts and were now available to a large number of people. The interest shown by the humanists was not, however, limited to written sources: they also researched ancient coins, sculptures, and above all the architecture of Antiquity. This comprehensive study of the culture of Antiquity led many scholars to break away from medieval theological and philosophical ideas. The humanists formulated a new image of man: now man stood center stage as the pinnacle of creation. These new ideas spread among the architects too. One such opinion, put forward by Vitruvius and taken up again in the Renaissance, was that human proportions were the measure of all things. The figure of a man describing the geometrical forms of a circle and a square, as recorded by Leonardo da Vinci as well, can be found in numerous drawings of the period.

In the fourteenth century Italy experienced a major economic upturn, its cities grew rapidly, and out of this a mercantile class emerged. Alongside the Church and princely courts they constituted the most important patrons for artists and architects. At this time Florence became one of the richest city states in Italy. Several great mercantile and banking families ruled the city republic, and as architectural clients they also shaped the face of the city. The Renaissance began in Florence in the early fifteenth century and the architecture of this time was dominated above all by Filippo Brunelleschi (1377–1446). The Florentine architect brought radical innovations to many building projects in his native city. The double-shell construction of the dome of Florence's cathedral, Santa Maria del Fiore, which Brunelleschi embarked upon in 1420, already offered an idea of his approach to architectural problems, an approach which was as self-confident as it was undogmatic (see also pp. 34/35).

left—**Leonardo da Vinci, Vitruvian Man** | Accademia, Venice.

1404 – 1472 Leon Battista Alberti

"The architects of the Renaissance trusted in the dimensions and harmony of geometric forms."

Even at the start of his career Brunelleschi abandoned the building forms and traditions which had been handed down from the Gothic period. Instead he looked back at the architecture of ancient temples whose ruins he had studied in detail in Rome. One of Brunelleschi's first projects of 1419, the design for the Ospedale degli Innocenti, a foundlings' home for orphans, shows a clear reference system of architectural elements both horizontally and vertically. The building is laid out around a symmetrical axis which starts at the entrance, and clear proportions determine the building's parts. This is also demonstrated in the loggia of the foundlings' home: its nine arches supported by slender Corinthian columns run the length of the entrance side of the building. The vaulted arcade is based on a square ground-plan, and this basic form in turn determines the measurements of the nine bays, their width, height, and depth (fig. p. 75). Balanced proportions create a harmonious and peaceful impression of space—completely different from Gothic buildings, which were dominated by the principle of verticality. Brunelleschi trusted in the dimensions and harmony of geometric

right—**Filippo Brunelleschi, Church of Santo Spirito** | Florence, begun in 1434.

c. **1455**—Gutenberg invents the printing press ·············· **1478**—The Spanish Inquisition is established··· **RENAISSANCE ARCHITECTURE 72/73**

1453—Fall of Constantinople···

1492—Columbus's first voyage to America

1506—First stone laying of St Peter's Basilica in Rome····· **RENAISSANCE ARCHITECTURE** **74/75**
1506—First stone laying of St Peter's Basilica in Rome·····1517—Beginning of Reformation (Martin Luther's *95 Theses*)·····

1510—Nicolaus Copernicus develops his heliocentric cosmology·····

1508–1580 Andrea Palladio

forms, countering the light-filled shell of the Gothic cathedral with harmoniously structured spaces and surfaces, which relate to each other in a mutually balanced way.

In 1434 Brunelleschi began building work on the Church of Santo Spirito, also in Florence, which he created as a three-nave cruciform basilica with a flat ceiling (fig. pp. 72/73). The proportions of the entire building are based on the square described by the crossing, the point where the nave and transept intersect. All the measurements within the church proceed from this basic module; the spatial relationships of all parts in the entire structure are clearly set up according to this. In the nave, the wall of the central aisle, the lower arcade, and the fenestrated upper part of the wall occupy approximately the same amount of space, which intensifies the overall impression of harmony. Large, glazed walls or detailed architectural ornamentation are nowhere to be seen—the age of the Gothic cathedrals is long past. In Santo Spirito it is the impression of symmetrical space which dominates, articulated by the gray composition of architectural elements and surmounted by a central dome.

The strict emphasis on form, the symmetrical ground-plan, and the regular articulation of the façade became predominant elements in the architecture of the Renaissance. This is also evident in the urban palaces which appeared in Florence and other cities in the fifteenth century. For the banker and politician Giovanni Rucellai, architect Leon Battista Alberti (1404–72) designed a three-story palazzo, which was built around the middle of the century and whose articulation could not have been expressed more clearly (fig. left). The three stories of the building are separated from each other by cornices. The vertical organization of the façade offers an unambiguous quotation from Antiquity: here Alberti was following the classical orders of the ancient world, as shown on the Colosseum in Rome, for example. Indeed while flat wall spaces rather than columns compose the front of the Palazzo Rucellai, the three levels nevertheless remain the same: on the lower story Alberti uses the Doric order, above it the Ionic, and on the top story the Corinthian order. The image is one of clear proportions and symmetry. Alberti was convinced that beauty was a question of mathematical calculation, as he wrote: "The same numbers, by means of which the agreement of sounds affects our ears with delight, are the very same which please our eyes and our minds."

Alberti was also one of the first theorists to emphasize a scientific approach to architecture and art.

left—**LEON BATTISTA ALBERTI, PALAZZO RUCELLAI** | Florence | 1453.

above—**FILIPPO BRUNELLESCHI, OSPEDALE DEGLI INNOCENTI** Florence | 1419.

1526—Completion of St Peter's Basilica in Rome ·· 1555—Peace of Augsburg, ending religious struggles during Reformation ·······························

1556–1629 Carlo Mader

"Artists and architects were no longer seen as craftsmen but belonged to the ranks of the scholars."

representation of perspective was developed by Filippo Brunelleschi, who thereby enhanced his reputation as more than just an architect. Brunelleschi's rules on perspective were translated into an image by the painter Masaccio (1401–28). His fresco of *The Holy Trinity* in the church of Santa Maria Novella in Florence shows a barrel-vaulted space represented using the illusionistic means of a perspectival construction of space (fig. left). The converging lines of the architecture meet at a point, which lies at the height of the kneeling patrons, who are located outside in front of the architectural niche. This new knowledge about proportion and perspective was also written down: the artist Piero della Francesca (c. 1420–92) addressed the question of perspective for painting in a treatise; and Alberti, the universal man, presented the scientific basis of painting in his work *Della pittura* [On Painting], which was published around 1435/36. Numerous artists and theorists now debated questions about painting and sculpture, bringing art and science together. One result of this combination was the new social position of the artist: now he was no longer seen as a craftsman but belonged to the ranks of the scholars. And the same went for the architect: during the Renaissance, architecture too became the subject of theoretical convergences, and architects earned their new place in society. Architect and theorist Alberti described their role as creators

For example, when researching representation using perspective he enlisted the help of mathematics. In the end representation with a central perspective became the dominant form in the Renaissance. Now artists were able to render a three-dimensional space on the two dimensions of the canvas by means of illusionistic representation. Behind this lay the discovery that all lines that run at right angles to the picture plane meet at a vanishing point in the center of the picture. Figures and objects in this space were now no longer represented larger or smaller according to their importance in the action of the painting, but according to their position in the depth of space— and consequently in proportion. This new pictorial

1564—Birth of Galileo Galilei · 1595—Premiere of Shakespeare's *Romeo and Juliet* · · · **RENAISSANCE ARCHITECTURE** **76/77**
1570—Birth of Guy Fawkes ·
1571—Birth of Johannes Kepler ·

1598–1680 Gian Lorenzo Bernini

of the human environment, and in 1452 the humanist wrote in his work *De re aedificatoria* [On the Art of Building in Ten Books]: "Architecture is a great thing, which cannot be undertaken by all. One must have intelligence, and persevering zeal, the best knowledge and long practice, and above all grave and severe judgement and counsel to succeed in the profession of architect. For in matters of building the first glory of all is to judge well that which is fitting. To build, in fact, is a necessity. To build conveniently responds to necessity and utility, but to build so that one is praised by men of glory and not criticized by the frugal, can only come from the ability of a learned, wise and judicious artist." In complete contrast to the medieval architect, who only rarely committed the design of a building to paper, now the overall planning took place at the beginning of the process. Ground-plans,

elevations, sections, and perspectival drawings of the building provided a comprehensive graphic rendering and offered the possibility of trying out different building forms in the first instance on paper. Even the master-planning of entire cities was now carried out according to the principles of Renaissance architecture. Alberti addressed the theme of the ideal city, with the emphasis on strict proportionality and adherence to rules. Urban regeneration projects were undertaken both as debates on paper, and in the form of built architecture (fig. above). Referring to Vitruvius's treatise on architecture, Alberti had formulated that every architectural design had three requirements in order to be correct: for every building he demanded commodity (*commodità*), firmness (*perpetuità*), and finally the built object must also possess beauty or delight (*bellezza*).

left—**MASACCIO, THE HOLY TRINITY** | fresco | 1426 – 28 | Santa Maria Novella, Florence.
above—**CENTRAL ITALIAN ARTIST, VIEW OF AN IDEAL CITY** | end of the 15th century | Galleria Nazionale delle Marche, Urbino.
next double page spread—**LEON BATTISTA ALBERTI, FAÇADE OF SANTA MARIA NOVELLA** | Florence | 1458.

c. 105—Invention of paper in China .... **476**—End of the Western Roman Empire ....

.... **c. 150**—Ptolemy develops his geocentric cosmology ....

.... **216**—Completion of the Baths of Caracalla in Rome ....

80/81

442–537 Isidore of Miletus   2nd half of the 5th C. – before 558 Anthemius of Tralles

SYMMETRY FIRST: THE CENTRALLY PLANNED BUILDING

Medieval churches were almost invariably based on longitudinal ground-plans, which usually took the form of a cross. In Romanesque and Gothic building in particular this directional structure was the usual form for sacred architecture. But it was by no means the only form: during all historical periods buildings were also created on the basis of a symmetrical ground-plan. In these centrally planned buildings all the elements are related to a central point, and unlike basilicas these buildings have no clear orientation. The central ground-plan can take the form of a circle, a polygon, or a square—even a Greek cross with four arms of equal length can be the basic form of a centrally planned building.

More than any other period in history, it was the Renaissance which saw the greatest artistic flowering of the ideal of the centrally planned building. But the story of the centrally planned building also starts with a work of Roman architecture: its culmination is ultimately represented by the Pantheon in Rome (see also pp. 30–32). This circular building was built between 118 and 125 A.D. and surmounted with

a massive dome. The Pantheon remained in use even after the Roman period as a Christian church, and today numbers among the best preserved monuments of ancient Rome.

In early Christian architecture it was mainly baptisteries and tombs which were built on a round or polygonal footprint. The commonly used octagonal ground-plan can be seen, for example, in the church of San Vitale in Ravenna, which was built in the sixth century. A similarly octagonal dome with a diameter of 16 meters covers the central space (figs. left and above). An ambulatory surrounds the

left—**SAN VITALE** | Ravenna | mid 6th century | view of interior of the dome.

right—**SAN VITALE** | view of the cupola.

82/83 CENTRALLY PLANNED BUILDING ·········· **800**—Charlemagne is crowned emperor ·············· **1096**—Beginning of the First Crusade

976—Construction of St Mark's Basilica in Venice ············

1010—First stone laying of St Michael's Church in Hildesheim

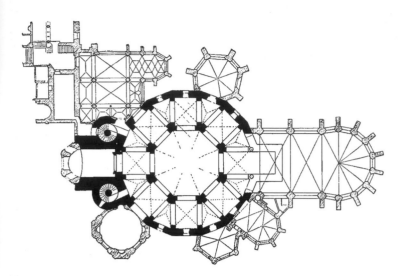

octagon, which is lit by round-headed windows, and which leads into the interior through similarly high round arches. This ambulatory extends over two stories, and in the upper story there are galleries which in turn are enclosed by semi-domes. The pictorial decoration of the dome with its *trompe-l'oeil* paintings was created in the early modern period. However, the floral and ornamental mosaics that cover the floor and the altar area of the church still date from the sixth century.

Occasionally the original central ground-plan of a building disappeared as a result of later modifications and can no longer be recognized at first sight. This is the case in the Palatine Chapel in Aachen, Germany, which was built on an octagonal ground-plan (figs. above and right). Since its creation in 790 the church has been restructured many times and today the octagon forms the center of Aachen Cathedral. Originally the small church was part of Charlemagne's imperial palace. For the rulers of the early medieval period, who had no fixed residence but continually traveled around their empire, these palaces were places to live and conduct the business of government, serving to consolidate their power at the same time. Most imperial palaces are only known through archeological excavations, and of the building in Aachen too, only the chapel remains. The main room which is enclosed by a dome is a

two-story octagon just 20 meters in diameter, attached to the choir in the east. The octagon opens up through arches leading to the vaulted, 16-sided ambulatory. Charlemagne's throne stood in the upper church: the emperor was crowned in Aachen and also chose the Palatine Chapel as his burial place. The centrally planned building remained a common architectural form as a tomb or baptistery. Up until the age of Classicism it offered an alternative to the cross-shaped church ground-plan. During the Renaissance interest in the culture of Antiquity inspired the rediscovery of Vitruvius's books on architecture from the first century B.C. The Roman architectural theorist had thoroughly researched ideal proportions and had found them in the forms of the circle and the square. Thus, he concluded, these fundamental forms should also be the original forms for temple buildings. Renaissance architects adopted the strictly geometrical ground-plans in the form of a circle or square, considering them to be the epitome of symmetry. For architectural theorist Leon Battista Alberti (1404–72) the centrally planned building was an image of divine order. As a result centrally

above—**PALATINE CHAPEL AACHEN** | c. 790–800 | ground-plan.
right—**PALATINE CHAPEL AACHEN** | view of interior of the octagon.

84/85 CENTRALLY PLANNED BUILDING ·········**c. 1115**—Construction of Angkor Wat················ **1526**—Completion of St Peter's Basilica in Rome
·················**1307–1321**—Dante Alighieri writes the *Divine Comedy* ·················
·················**c. 1455**—Gutenberg invents the printing press·················

1404–1472 Leon Battista Alberti   1444–1514 Donato Bramante   1508–1580 Andrea Palladio

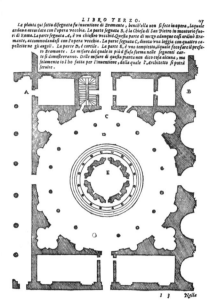

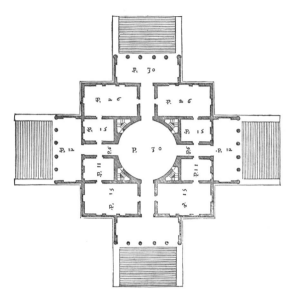

planned buildings played a major role in Renaissance church building. At the same time it did not go unnoticed that with the central ground-plan reference was being made to ancient—and therefore—pagan temples, such as the Pantheon for example, and thus was in competition to the basilica with its basic form of a cross composed of a nave and transept.

One of the first people who put into practice the knowledge derived from the study of the centrally planned buildings of Antiquity was Donato Bramante (1444–1514). Originally his small round temple in Rome, the Tempietto of S. Pietro in Montorio, was intended to form the center of an equally circular courtyard. However this idea was not realized: it remained a round building located in a square courtyard, but the architect Sebastiano Serlio (1475–1554) preserved the idea as a drawing in his *Seven Books of Architecture* (fig. above left).

In the Renaissance the centrally planned form was not only of renewed interest in church building, but it was also being debated beyond the realm of sacred architecture. Following the architecture of Antiquity, architects took inspiration from the central ground-plan in their designs for secular buildings as well. Andrea Palladio (1508–80), the most sought-after villa architect in the Veneto, took the country houses of the ancient world as his model. When the well-off Venetians in the sixteenth century discovered the

advantages of country living beyond the lagoon, Palladio built suitable villas for them, drawing on models from the architecture of Antiquity. One of his clients was Paolo Almerico, who moved back to the mainland of the Veneto at the end of his professional career in Rome. Palladio built La Rotonda for him, thus creating a building that would continue to have great influence until the age of Classicism (fig. right). Almerico's country residence was begun in 1566 outside the city of Vicenza, and owes its name to the circular hall surmounted by a dome which is located in the exact center of the villa. With La Rotonda Palladio realized the idea of the perfect centrally planned building: further salons are arranged symmetrically around the domed central hall according to the strictly square ground-plan. The entrance too follows ancient models: Palladio designed it as a temple frontage—this was extremely daring for a secular building. Six Ionic columns support the triangular pediment, which is decorated with sculptures. Symmetry was the greatest requirement here, too, and as a result Palladio was not content with creating the entrance façade as a temple frontage, but he also placed similar porticos on all four sides of the building. By dispensing with a main view, and instead affording the same importance to all the building's axes, Palladio emphasized the symmetry of the architecture.

far left—**Sebastiano Serlio, Ground-plan of the Tempietto of San Pietro in Montorio** | *Seven Books of Architecture*
book 3 | Venice | 1540 | fol. 41.
left—**Andrea Palladio, La Rotonda** | Vicenza | 1566–69
ground-plan.
above—**La Rotonda** | Vicenza | 1566–69.

1508–1580 Andrea Palladio   1556–1629 Carlo Maderno

BAROQUE BUILDINGS: ARCHITECTURE IN MOTION

Symmetrical, clearly articulated buildings with harmoniously proportioned interiors and façades were the declared goal of the architects of the Renaissance. The architects of the Baroque, by contrast, no longer believed in the equal status of individual elements, but emphasized the effect of the whole. Art in the period between 1580 and 1770 was summed up in the word Baroque. At this time the Catholic Church was the most important patron, and as a result it was church building which advanced the Baroque style to the greatest extent. In the wake of the Reformation, which Martin Luther's Theses had initiated in 1517, the Catholic Church was called into question. Now the Church wanted to strengthen its role in society once again, in addition representing itself through architecture. As a result churches and monasteries arose in the Catholic countries of Europe whose aim was to convince the faithful of the importance of the Church.

The Baroque style began in Rome. It was there, towards the end of the sixteenth century, that modernizing urban planning reached its peak: whole streets were laid out and the Vatican was incorporated architecturally into the city. The newly built

St. Peter's Basilica, the most important church in Christendom, inaugurated a major project in Rome at the beginning of the century (fig. pp. 88–89). Over the long period of its construction this project went through many changes of plan and architect, finally becoming one of the most striking examples of Baroque architecture.

When the new building started under Pope Julius II in 1506, a building on a central plan was mapped out which architects carried out over the following decades. Forty years later, Michelangelo Buonarroti (1475–1564) surmounted the church with a massive dome. Two elements determine its external impact: the repeating motif of paired columns and, set back from them, the straight-headed, pedimented windows. These forms alternate below the monumental dome, which seems to be put in motion through this variation. On the dome, too, Michelangelo created optical depth and relief: across its shell, ribs radiate forth like light rays from the dome's lantern. Between them are set more windows, which pursue the pediment motif of the drum. By repeating individual elements, but varying them, Michelangelo played with the effect of nearness and distance, here too creating the impression of movement in spite of the heaviness of the dome.

By 1590 the centrally planned building was finally finished according to plan, but the project of

left—GIAN LORENZO BERNINI, ST. PETER'S SQUARE | Rome | 1656–67.

88/89 BAROQUE BUILDINGS .... **1618**—Beginning of the Thirty Years' War .... **1649**—Oliver Cromwell turns England into a Commonwealth
.... **1632**—Construction of Taj Mahal ....
.... **1648**—End of the Thirty Years' War ....

St. Peter's was nonetheless a long way from completion. Baroque architect Carlo Maderno (c. 1556–1629) was given the task of continuing the work. At the beginning of the seventeenth century he was required to add a nave to the central ground-plan. In the Baroque period the directional nave structure was once again acquiring more supporters: not only did it offer more space, but with its basic form of a cross it also came closer to the architectural task of a Christian church. When St. Peter's nave was finished in 1626, however, the building was no longer convincing in its effect: the dome had lost its monumentality, and by contrast the façade looked too wide for its height. In order to return once again to the originally planned effect, it was decided to re-design the entire square in front of the church. Gian Lorenzo Bernini (1598–1680) created an oval square that demonstrates the whole sense of movement of the Italian Baroque. He planned two squares, one after the other: the *piazza obliqua* forms an oval positioned at right-angles that culminates in the trapezoid *piazza retta*, helping St. Peter's to create its effect as the end-point and climax of this site. Wide colonnades embrace the square like two arms and emphasize the momentum of the site created by open and closed forms. In addition Bernini lent the architecture an upward movement optically by increasing the height of the colonnades around the square as they approach the church.

Dynamism, momentum, animation: these central characteristics of Baroque architecture are not only employed in the project of St. Peter's Basilica. The dynamic formal language typical of the Baroque can also be seen in many other of the numerous new churches and church rebuildings of the period. One of them is the church of Sant'Andrea al Quirinale in Rome, also designed by Bernini (p. 90 fig. above left). The form of its ground-plan is new and would be used again and again during the Baroque period. The church is based on a transverse oval and this form recurs many times in the body of the building. Thus the dome too has a basic oval form and as a result the drum leading to it is also oval in shape. The curved forms continue on the outside of the building: curved steps lead up to the entrance, which is enclosed by a round roof. Even the walls adjoining the portal take part in the movement, as they are curved and jut out some distance. And it was not only the façades of Baroque buildings that seemed to move and pulsate in concave and convex curves. The ground-plans too occasionally contribute to the dynamic effect: the footprint of Sant'Ivo alla Sapienza, the church of the University of Rome, is a six-pointed star whose differently shaped points create an optical interplay. Francesco Borromini (1599–1667) began work on the new building in 1642 and the project was to continue for over 20 years. The resulting interior is a space which seems to curve forwards and back. This impression is created in Sant'Ivo by the ends of the star-shaped ground-plan: they are extended alternately either into niches which are rounded on the outside or into enclosures which curve inwards on the inside (p. 90 fig. above right).

Decoration, in the interior as well as on the façade, was thus an important component of Baroque architecture. On the façades of Baroque buildings, architectural ornamentation provided effects of light

above—**MICHELANGELO, ST. PETER'S BASILICA** | Rome | dome 1547 – 90.
right—**ST. PETER'S BASILICA** | interior view.

·········· **1689**—Bill of Rights in England ··· **1769**—Invention of the steam engine

······························ **726**—Jonathan Swift publishes *Gulliver's Travels* ·····································

··· **1756**—Birth of Mozart··

1732–1808 Carl Gotthard Langhans   **1750–1789 Abraham Darby**   **1763–1828 Pierre-Alexandre Vignon**

and shadow and thus contributed to the impression of movement. In the interiors too—in churches as in secular buildings—decoration knew no limits. Ceilings and walls disappeared behind stucco ornament and painting, and magnificent marble fittings, columns with richly ornamented capitals, or lavishly designed floors completed the splendid overall effect. Even the fittings of Baroque churches were designed for effect: the interior with its marble, gold, and rich figurative decoration became more and more complex, as illusionistic wall and ceiling paintings contributed further to lending the spaces volume and depth. Frequently this was more appearance than reality: marble was frequently used merely as a veneer and columns were in reality made of brick; mirrors gave a false sense of size which a small room could certainly not compete with; or domes which looked magnificent on the outside were constructed with a simple wooden framework on the inside. Sometimes the perspectively correct painted architecture looked like a continuation of what had actually been built. This is shown in the ceiling fresco of the church of Sant'Ignazio in Rome, which was painted in the 1690s. The painter Andrea Pozzo (1642–1709) fused architecture and painting together on the ceiling of the church (fig. right). His columns and arches painted in the vault of the ceiling look real at first sight and form a continuation of the

actual architecture one story higher. The illusionistic architecture fulfills its purpose and provides the illusion of a wide space filled with movement. Painting and architecture come together to trick the viewer's perception through stylized illusionism. This trend was not limited to sacred architecture any more than the wealth of forms or opulence: secular buildings from the Baroque period, such as palaces or city residences, were no less magnificent in their appearance (see also The First Palaces, pp. 94–101).

above left—**GIAN LORENZO BERNINI, SANT'ANDREA AL QUIRINALE** Rome | 1658–61.
above right—**FRANCESCO BORROMINI, SANT'IVO ALLA SAPIENZA** | Rome interior view.
right—**ANDREA POZZO, SANT'IGNAZIO** | Rome | ceiling fresco | 1691–94.
next double page spread—**SANTA MARIA MAGGIORE** | Rome | interior view.

1506—Construction of St Peter's Basilica in Rome ···· 1519—Construction of Château de Chambord ·······································

1510—Nicolaus Copernicus develops his heliocentric cosmology ··

1517—Beginning of Reformation (Martin Luther's *95 Theses*)······································

94/95

1508–1580 Andrea Palladio

THE FIRST PALACES

No absolute ruler wanted to do without the suitable architectural expression of his importance. Magnificent palaces were required to shore up a monarch's claim to validity in an appropriate fashion—throughout Europe. The prototype of the absolute ruler, Louis XIV, reigned in splendor in his monumental palace at Versailles just outside Paris. All its surroundings, the town as well as the countryside, were oriented towards the palace. Soon similar palaces appeared in Vienna and Madrid, Turin and Potsdam, where Baroque palace complexes grew up following the style of Versailles. They wanted to catch up with the French model, sometimes even imitating the scale of the building project. Palace building was, after the impressive churches and monasteries of the Baroque period, the most important architectural task of the seventeenth and eighteenth centuries. Up until that time the royal residence had been the castle. Throughout the Middle Ages, castle complexes had also always been defensive buildings with massive masonry and battlements. Gradually these two architectural tasks developed into separate buildings. Fortifications were now appropriate for defense, while the royal residence now had one task

above all others: to be prestigious. The royal residences of the sixteenth century demonstrate this transition. The Château de Chambord in the Loire Valley in France, for example, is in many respects more like a castle (fig. left). The French king, François I, commissioned it as his new hunting lodge. Like the residential towers of medieval castles the prominent central building of the four-winged complex stands out, emphasizing the character of the palace as fortification. Even the four massive round towers look more like the defensive towers of a castle than palace architecture. And finally the roof profile, with its forest of towers and chimneys, underlines Chambord's impression of fortification. Meanwhile the journey from castle to palace was undertaken by the Louvre in Paris too—and since then it has changed from a royal residence into one of the greatest museums in the world (fig. p. 97). The Louvre was built at the end of the twelfth century as a rectangular fort with one separate, round tower. In the sixteenth century, under François I, who was a lover of Italian Renaissance architecture, a palace appropriate to the period was to be created out of the medieval castle. He planned a complex of four wings each with two stories, which would also be partially built over the next decades. Under King Louis XIV, however, building work at the Louvre came to a temporary standstill. Royal interest in another building

left—Domenico da Cortona et al., Château de Chambord 1519–50.

1555—Peace of Augsburg, ending religious struggles during Reformation

1570—Birth of Guy Fawkes..**1595**—Premiere of Shakespeare's *Romeo and Juliet*

c. **1580**—Beginning of the Baroque period

1556–1629 Carlo Maderno

project stood in the way of the further extension of the former castle. The new Palace of Versailles soon replaced the Louvre as the royal residence, and established completely new ideas in palace building.

Until well into the eighteenth century, France set the standards in palace building. And the absolutist residence *par excellence* was the Palace of Versailles. When the self-styled Sun King, Louis XIV, ascended to the French throne at the age of 23, France was the new European superpower. In 1682 Louis moved his court from Paris to the nearby hitherto insignificant village of Versailles. The king involved the nobles closely in the ceremonial life of the court, thus leaving them no time for political ambitions. In so doing he thwarted potential opponents, while simultaneously reinforcing the dissociation of the monarch from the people. An extravagant royal household on the one hand and strict etiquette on the other characterized the court of Versailles in equal measure. The ingenious hierarchy of the court and the use of courtly ceremonies as a system of communication within the nobility required appropriate architectural structures. Not least, these structures had to demonstrate that the king was the center of everything, as Louis's motto had it: "L'état, c'est moi." The king was not simply the focus of the state, he was the state itself. He tried to show this in the

above left—**Pierre Patel, View of the Château and Garden of Versailles** | 1668 | oil on canvas | 115 × 161 cm | Musée du Château, Versailles.
above right—**Louis Le Vau et al., The Marble Court** | Versailles.
right—**The Louvre** | Paris.

urban layout of Versailles too: at the center of the site is the palace to which everything is oriented in a star pattern, indicating that all roads lead to the king. The building of France's new center of power began in 1668 in the middle of a rather inhospitable area west of Paris. There Louis bought the village of Trianon and commissioned architect Louis Le Vau (1612–70) to develop the old Versailles hunting lodge to monumental dimensions. The façade of the new palace alone was to extend over 600 meters, designed in the French Baroque style that was named for the monarch and became known as Louis XIV style. Prestige was the watchword in the design of the palace and its garden as well as in the magnificent decoration of its spacious suites of rooms.

The first stage of building, the enveloping of the old palace, was finished two years after building work began, and the park-like garden was already taking shape. However it would still take a good 50 years before the last room, the royal chapel, was completed.

·········· **1618–1648**—Thirty Years' War ·· **1649**—Oliver Cromwell turns England into a Commonwealth··· **PALACES** 96/97

1632—Construction of Taj Mahal ····································

········· **1644**—Beginning of the Qing Dynasty in China·········

1599–1667 Francesco Borromini   1646–1708 Jules Hardouin-Mansart   1612–1670 Louis le Vau

"Diverse palaces in Italy, Spain, Germany, and Austria followed the French model given by Versailles – the building intended to make people aware of the divine legitimacy of the ruler."

1662–1736 Matthäus Daniel Pöppelmann

In the meantime the architect Jules Hardouin-Mansart (1646–1708) had taken over architectural direction. He built the south and north wings, which enclose the Court of Honor alongside the main building which is set back (fig. p. 96 top right). On the first floor of the palace Hardouin-Mansart emphasized the prestigious character of the palace complex with his Hall of Mirrors. This hall, 71 meters in length, was located on the garden side and provided the proper context for court balls and grandiose receptions. Around the hill on which the Palace of Versailles was built, the king had a no less impressive garden landscape designed on an area of over 800 hectares under the direction of royal gardener André Le Nôtre (1613–1700): entire woods were planted and canals dug to keep the numerous fountains and water jets running. Paths led symmetrically through the park, which was strewn with statues and marble vases. Around the palace, geometrically shaped beds formed the parterre, and perfectly straight rows of pruned trees and sculptural topiary hedges characterized the overall picture. Nature was rigorously transformed and adapted to fit the total work of art that was the Palace of Versailles.

At end of the seventeenth century, although Versailles was not quite finished, the palace complex began to be quoted or copied by the absolute monarchs of Europe. In many places, palace buildings in the Versailles style were intended to make people aware of the divine legitimacy of the ruler.

right—Matthäus Daniel Pöppelmann, Zwinger Palace | Dresden 1697–1716.

1732–1808 Carl Gotthard Langhans

················· **1756**—Birth of Mozart ·· **1789–1799**—French Revolution··· **PALACES** 100/101
·· **1774**—Goethe writes *The Sorrows of Young Werther*····················
·· **1776**—Declaration of Independence in the USA···················

1750– 1789 Abraham Darby

Italy, Spain, Germany, and Austria followed the French model. Be it Nymphenburg Palace in Munich or the magnificent Belvedere and Schönbrunn Palace complexes in Vienna, Versailles was the perfect model for the palace of the absolute monarch (fig. above). The idea of the total work of art, or *Gesamtkunstwerk*, in which all artistic genres operated together, extended throughout the Baroque period. It was by no means limited to architecture and the fine arts, but rather artists played out courtly life using music and costumes in theatrical productions or operas. The Baroque prince, Augustus the Strong, indulged his penchant for courtly celebrations even to the extent of building an open-air ballroom in the Zwinger Palace in Dresden (fig. pp. 98/99). Architect Matthäus Daniel

Pöppelmann (1662–1736) arranged the pavilions and galleries symmetrically around the almost square inner courtyard, while to the west the Kronentor, like a triumphal arch, forms the main entrance. The center of the broad inner courtyard is indicated by four fountains, from which four axes radiate, leading to the pavilions. As a total work of art in the spirit of the late Baroque every part of the Zwinger, every staircase and façade, is decorated: stone vases adorn the garden, and *putti*, masks, and garlands cover the surfaces of the walls. The interplay of architecture, sculpture, and ornament forms the backdrop-like character of the Dresden palace complex. All artistic genres operated together to provide the absolute ruler with the proper framework for his self-dramatization.

left—SALA TERRENA, UPPER BELVEDERE | Vienna.
above—JOHANN LUKAS VON HILDEBRANDT, GARDEN FAÇADE OF THE
UPPER BELVEDERE | Vienna | 1721–23.

WOOD? STONE? IRON!

It was neither wood nor stone but iron that made the bridge at Coalbookdale, and it was constructed in an iron foundry. The Iron Bridge, named for its pioneering architectural achievement, can be found in Coalbrookdale in the west of England. It was there, where the town meets the River Severn, that the first cast-iron bridge was constructed in 1777. The metal was not, however, unknown: iron had already been used in Greek and Roman Antiquity in the form of nails or brackets, and in Gothic architecture it was used to reinforce the frames of the great cathedral windows. However, in the eighteenth century iron took on a wholly new function: once seen in a supporting role, iron itself was now considered as a material for building. The simplified manufacture of iron heralded this change: if, previously, large amounts of charcoal were needed to smelt iron from ore, in the ore and coal mines of Coalbrookdale they succeeded in replacing the ever more scarce charcoal with cheaper coke. As a result, the production of cast iron increased rapidly. In the end ferries were not enough to transport the increasing amounts of iron across the River Severn, and so a bridge had to be built (fig. p. 104).

Architect Thomas Pritchard designed the bridge in the material it was built to transport, cast iron. The Iron Bridge spans the river over a length of thirty meters. Five slim iron ribs run between masonry abutments and support the road crossing. Abraham Darby and John Wilkinson cast these iron ribs in two separate halves, a method which offered advantages for the technical completion of the bridge: the iron sections were completely assembled in situ within just three months.

Thus cast iron was introduced as a construction material. Gothic was still the formal language, as the linear framework of the arches of the bridge indicates. But in terms of the use of iron the bridge at Coalbrookdale, which still stands to this day, is a first. And it went from strength to strength: the Coalbrookdale foundry received numerous orders modelled on the 1777 bridge, and the iron ribs were shipped all over the country. Here the Iron Bridge was only the beginning, and in the course of the nineteenth century, iron would develop into an indispensable material. Soon not just cast iron but also wrought iron that could better withstand tensile forces could be produced in larger quantities. Iron could be held back no longer: it was cheap to produce, and flexible to manipulate as it could be either wrought or cast. Britain was the home of the Industrial Revolution, and even in the nineteenth century it was a

left—**Joseph Paxton, The Crystal Palace** | London | 1851.

1732 – 1808 Carl Gotthard Langhans

"From the eighteenth century, iron was used as a material for building – and soon developed into an indispensable material."

leading power in terms of trade and commerce. Unsurprisingly, then, people wanted to present the achievements of industry in an exhibition. The idea for the Great Exhibition of the Works of Industry of All Nations came to fruition in London around the middle of the century. Ultimately it was given the name of the first World's Fair and many others would follow in its wake. But for the premiere in 1851 it was decided to build a large exhibition hall in London's Hyde Park. The idea of the British architect Joseph Paxton (1803–65) gained favor after an international competition to design it produced no result. His architectural approach was groundbreaking. Paxton created a glass palace, using in its construction the new materials of iron and glass. The Crystal Palace was 564 meters in length—or 1,851 feet, a playful reference to the year of the exhibition. The hall-like glass arcade was divided crossways by a raised, barrel-vaulted transept. At its highest point the glass

exhibition hall was as much as forty meters high and thus functioned as a shell containing the huge trees in Hyde Park. The cast-iron frame of the Crystal Palace was supported by thin columns between which a glass skin was inserted: in total Paxton enclosed an area of almost seven hectares with his Crystal Palace. The space within the glass shell was further divided up according to the exhibitors and products being shown (fig. p. 102).
This London exhibition building was a milestone in iron and glass architecture. Around the middle of the century a whole area of experimentation in building with new materials emerged: greenhouses made of glass and iron became fashionable, Paxton himself being an early builder of such plant houses. In their formal language these constructions were not new. But in light of the materials used, cast iron and glass, such construction marked a break and showed how far iron architecture had developed since the first iron bridge in Coalbrookdale. With the Crystal Palace a great public building was created—indeed a national advertisement—out of nothing but an iron skeleton and fragile glass. Contemporary observers thought highly of the glass palace and the building was the central attraction of the whole exhibition: "All over the world people were talking of nothing else but the industrial exhibition in London and of the wonderful glass palace with its

left—**THOMAS PRITCHARD AND ABRAHAM DARBY, THE IRON BRIDGE** England | 1777.
above—**EXTERIOR VIEW OF THE CRYSTAL PALACE** | London | 1951 etching.
next double page spread—**PALM HOUSE IN KEW GARDENS** | London 1836–40.

"The new material brought with it many advantages: large expanses of space could be enclosed without the need for intrusive supports; and besides, iron was fire-proof."

hundred thousand columns, its high vaulted glass roof beneath which the tallest elms blossomed, and of its long central aisle whose end disappeared into the blue beyond." Aesthetically the Crystal Palace would reverberate until well into the twentieth century, as demonstrated not only by its imitators in other cities. The exhibition palace revealed the technical discoveries that great heights and roof spans did not have to be accompanied by massive stone architecture, and that support and wall could be separated. These discoveries can still be seen in the skeleton construction of twenty-first-century highrise buildings.

Paxton's Crystal Palace was also revolutionary in the way it was put together technically: many building components were manufactured in advance and just assembled in Hyde Park, with the result that a construction time *in situ* of just ten months was enough to erect the great exhibition building. Three thousand three hundred cast-iron columns, 2,224 girders, and 1,128 supports for the side galleries were delivered on time and assembled. The firm of Chance Brothers provided 84,000 square meters of glass, corresponding to a third of annual production in England at that time. Even contemporary commentators appreciated the idea of assembly as an important innovation, as the *Deutscher Magazin für Garten und Blumenkunde* reported in 1872: "The extraordinary significance of this undertaking, apart from the

short planning and construction times, lies above all in the process engineering, that is in the organization of labor which can be compared with modern conveyor-belt assembly and machine manufacture." The Crystal Palace was not only built in record time, but it was demolished even faster. It was not intended to be permanent but only to last for the six months' duration of the Hyde Park exhibition. The ease with which it could be dismantled had been an important criterion in the choice of design. Paxton's glass exhibition hall was thus taken apart in 1852, but reconstructed in a larger form in Sydenham, where, however, it was destroyed by fire in 1936.

As a result of the London World's Fair, iron construction really took off for the first time. An early catalyst in this process of development was the railway, which in less than twenty years during the nineteenth century became an important means of transport. The new steam engine proved to be the motivating means for locomotives. The railway brought about a change in the nature of transport and created the transportational requirements for the development of technology and industry. At the same time the construction of railway networks generated an enormous demand: iron, steel, and machinery were required for tracks and railway bridges, tunnels and steam engines. Iron construction is closely connected to the development of

1803–1865 Joseph Paxton

industrialization: the inhabitants of the fast-growing cities, for example, generated new building projects: railway stations burgeoned, as well as shopping arcades, markets, and exhibition halls. For iron architecture, bridge construction was merely a springboard, and the impetus from it was soon transferred to highrise building. Here a wide area opened up for the use of the new material, which brought with it many advantages.

In railway stations, for example, large expanses of space could be enclosed using iron, and without the need for intrusive supports (fig. above). Shopping arcades, which sprung up like mushrooms in European city centers, acquired through their iron-and-glass roofs protection from the elements, which still let the daylight in (fig. pp. 110/111). Iron columns and girders were used and roof trusses were made of cast iron, the fire-proof nature of the material bringing another major advantage.

In the late nineteenth century, steel moved into the fast lane and became a talking point as new dimensions in highrise buildings were discussed. For the load-bearing frameworks of skyscrapers, which emerged in the last years of the nineteenth century

in Chicago and New York, architects returned to the material (see also *Architecture that Scrapes the Sky*, pp. 114–125). In France the buildings of the Paris World's Fair became experiments in how to deal with the material. One such experiment was carried out by the engineer Gustave Eiffel (1832–1923) in 1889 on the occasion of the centenary celebrations of the French Revolution. The Eiffel Tower on the Champ de Mars, made of four pillars emerging from a square ground-plan which come together at the top, was almost three hundred meters tall (fig. pp. 112/113). Its visitors were assisted in their upward journey by another novelty—the elevator. After all, elevators had conquered in Europe just a few years before. Like the Crystal Palace forty years earlier, the Eiffel Tower was bolted together out of components *in situ*. Thus the construction period on the Champ de Mars was correspondingly short, despite the 12,000 individual parts used. The Eiffel Tower clearly demonstrates the building principle which lies at the heart of iron construction: a return to the principle of the timber-frame (fig. p. 112). The iron framework draws on traditional timber-frame construction, wherein horizontal, vertical, and diagonal beams and poles absorb the load forces and tensile forces. The amount of scepticism which the new material aroused, despite the well-known construction principle, can be seen in the mixture

above—THOMAS PROSSER ET AL., YORK STATION II | England | 1871–77.

............**1849**—Death of Chopin ....**1873**—Jules Verne publishes *Around the World in Eighty Days* ····· IRON **110/111**
................**1853 – 1856**—Crimean War ....**1861 – 1865**—American Civil War ···
.........................**1857 – 1859**—First world economic crisis ···

1867 – 1959 Frank Lloyd Wright   **1870 – 1947 Max Berg**   **1874 – 1954 Auguste Perret**

GIUSEPPE MENGONI, GALLERIA VITTORIO EMANUELE II | Milan
1865 – 67.

112 /113 IRON ············· **1876**—Invention of the telephone ·· **1889**—Completion of the Eiffel Tower ·············
1886—Completion of the Statue of Liberty ························
1883—First petrol-engined automobile ·····················

1881–1929 Adolf Meyer   1883–1969 Walter Gropius   1886–1969 Ludwig Mies van der Rohe

of derision and anxiety in the comments which the Eiffel Tower aroused in contemporaries even during its construction. Critics called the building a "tragic lamppost," and spoke of "a disgusting column of bolted tin." One resident of the Champ de Mars even initiated a law suit as he feared the Eiffel Tower might topple onto his house. Two million paying visitors, however, were not to be deterred and visited the steel tower during the six months of the World's Fair. Its lifespan was originally supposed to be limited to twenty months, but the Tower managed to avoid demolition. Ultimately it is not only the symbol of the

city, but also an attractive source of income: today the Eiffel Tower attracts some six million tourists every year.

The career of steel continued in similar fashion: since the end of the nineteenth century it has served primarily as a reinforcement for concrete and enjoyed another heyday in the raw concrete architecture of Le Corbusier (1887–1965), albeit concealed in precast concrete (see chapter Concrete, pp. 150–159). The high-tech architecture of the 1970s also showed an enthusiasm for steel: for example the Centre Pompidou in Paris displays the material openly.

above—**GUSTAVE EIFFEL, THE EIFFEL TOWER** | Paris | 1887–89
under construction.
right—**GUSTAVE EIFFEL, THE EIFFEL TOWER.**

····················**1857–1859**—First world economic crisis··· **1879**—Birth of Albert Einstein··· **114/115**
··· **1876**—Battle of the Little Bighorn·····························
··· **1877**—Leo Tolstoy publishes *Anna Karenina*·····························

1867–1959 Frank Lloyd Wright   **1874–1954 Auguste Perret**   **1883–1969 Walter Gropius**

ARCHITECTURE THAT SCRAPES THE SKY

Twentieth-century architecture is almost inconceivable without them: highrise buildings have risen to prominence over a very short period, making them for a long time the most sought-after building type worldwide. We can no longer imagine our cities without skyscapers. At the same time, their history is comparatively short and only begins towards the end of the nineteenth century. The word itself appeared in the 1880s: a building so high that it scraped the sky. In the first instance, highrise buildings came nowhere near the sky, having no more than six or seven stories. But these houses had to be accessed by stairs and this set height limits for building. In the mid-nineteenth century, however, the alternative to climbing stairs was invented: Elisha Otis (1811–61) introduced the first steam-driven passenger elevator. The problem of vertical transport had scarcely been solved, when buildings started to rise higher. Now, thanks to the elevator, the upper floors of a building were more sought-after than the lower. At first the buildings grew by only a few stories, but such modesty soon passed and the race for height drove highrise building onwards. At over eight hundred

meters high, the Burj Khalifa in Dubai established a new record in 2010.

The highrise changed the image of cities; Manhattan's skyline of skyscrapers is a prime example of this. The cult of the highrise did not, however, begin in New York, but in Chicago. The city on Lake Michigan in the northwest of the United States grew at an impressive speed in the last quarter of the nineteenth century, and by the turn of the century already numbered over a million inhabitants. The extension of the railroad lines around Chicago created the conditions for rapid industrial growth. While the city was preparing for a great boom, a fire destroyed a large area of the business district in 1871. Just a few weeks later, building began in a big way, and architectural renewal followed hard on its heels. New buildings had to fulfill two requirements: they should be able to be built quickly, and at the same time be good value for money. The area available in the chess-board-like grid of the city was limited and so new building had only one direction—they had to grow upwards. Soon people were talking about the "cloudscraper." At first they were primarily office buildings, one of which was the eleven-story Home Insurance Building, constructed between 1883 and 1885 (p. 116 fig. above left). Architect William LeBaron Jenney (1832–1907) used a load-bearing construction of steel and stone in his fifty-five-meter-high building. Where previously

116 / 117 SKYSCRAPERS ·············· **1887**—First Sherlock Homes novel is published ································· **1914**—Beginning of First World War···

1896—First modern Olympic Games···················

1906—San Francisco earthquake··········

1886–1969 Ludwig Mies van der Rohe   1895–1988 Ove Arup   1906–2005 Philip Johnson

massive masonry had supported the ceilings and exterior walls, now a skeleton of metal girders assumed this task. In this way the building gained in space: the thickness of the walls was reduced and by contrast valuable floor space was increased. Equally, the new way of building allowed for a greater expanse of windows. Compared with traditional masonry methods, the costs of steel-skeleton construction were considerably lower, in particular because the footprint of the building could be reduced. Above all, however, the building could be higher: "We are building to a height to rival the Tower of Babel," Jenney announced self-confidently as building work began. Despite all the innovation in construction, the building's façade imitated a formal language, which corresponded to a familiar way of building. The first highrises, which emerged in Chicago and a short time later in New York, sported somewhat historicizing façades. Wide ledges and powerful cornerstones recalled the role occupied originally by load-bearing heavy masonry. But such borrowings were only an intermediate step before a separate highrise aesthetic was established. What became accepted in central Chicago was the use of skeleton construction for highrise buildings. The Home Insurance Building no longer exists, but around the world skyscrapers refer back to this model of construction.

above left—WILLIAM LEBARON JENNEY, HOME INSURANCE BUILDING Chicago | 1883–85.
above center—BURNHAM AND ROOT, MASONIC TEMPLE | Chicago 1891–92.
above right—BURNHAM AND COMPANY, RELIANCE BUILDING | Chicago 1890–95.
right—WILLIAM VAN ALEN, CHRYSLER BUILDING | New York | 1928–30.

The development of the highrise should not be regarded separately from technical achievements: they could not have been built without passenger elevators, and only electric lighting and a sophisticated air-conditioning technology made the abundance of interior space useable. Meanwhile, Louis Sullivan (1856–1924) concerned himself with the theory of the next generation of buildings. The architect and theoretician embedded the skyscraper in a separate aesthetic: his conviction was "form follows function." "What is the chief characteristic of the tall office building?" he asked in his 1896 essay "The Tall Office Building Artistically Considered." He answered the question himself: "It must be tall, every inch of it tall. The force and power of altitude must be in it, the glory and pride of exaltation must be in it. It must be every inch a proud and soaring thing, rising in sheer

1922—Discovery of Tutankhamun's Tomb ·· 1946—First computer··· SKYSCRAPERS **118/119**
1925—Invention of television ·······················
1939–1945—Second World War ·············

b. 1917 Ieoh Ming Pei   b. 1935 Norman Foster   b. 1946 Daniel Libeskind

> *"In 1931 the Chrysler Building was deposed from its title as highest building in the world in favor of the Empire State Building."*

exultation that from bottom to top it is a unit without a single dissenting line."

After Chicago, the second great showplace for highrise architecture was New York. Its first skyscraper, the Fuller Building in Manhattan's Midtown, was built just after the turn of the century. Based on a triangular footprint, the structure is better known as the Flatiron Building, after the shape of its groundplan. Architect Daniel H. Burnham (1846–1912) also used familiar façade ornamentation in the terracotta covering of the steel frame. He built twenty-one stories to a height of eighty-seven meters, a world record at the time, true to his oft-cited credo: "Make no little plans. They have no magic to stir men's blood." This motto was also appropriate for the highrise architects who came after him in the city and who raised the records in quick succession. In 1928 the Big Apple saw the first skyscraper to exceed the height of one thousand feet: the Chrysler Building had seventy-seven stories and was 320 meters high when it was opened two years later (fig. p. 117). While the square base occupies the entire site, the volume of the building is reduced towards the top.

This "wedding-cake style" spread as a result of new building laws in New York in the 1920s: new buildings were only allowed unlimited height if their tower above the thirteenth floor occupied at most a quarter of the built base. Thus the Chrysler Building is a terraced pyramid, ending in a crown made of six arches placed one on top of the other on each side. Enthroned in splendor in the middle is a fifty-five-meter-high spire made of steel, which, however, could not prevent the Chrysler Building from being deposed from its title as highest building in the world as early as 1931 in favor of the Empire State Building. The entire building is a showcase for American modernity. Its façade is not historicist: on the contrary, it has a spire of high-grade steel, and is decorated with radiator grills and hub caps—the highrise embodied the automobile age. Architect William Van Alen (1882–1954) made reference to the building's commissioner, automobile tycoon Walter P. Chrysler, in the architectural ornamentation of the building. Soon after the economic crash of 1929 the architectural push upwards came to a temporary end. And when people started to build skyscrapers again, they looked completely different: instead of highrise towers with a base, mid-section, and spire, the post-World War II period saw the emergence of residential and office highrises in rectangular form. Pure steel constructions were reduced to a structural

left—**WILLIAM VAN ALEN, CHRYSLER BUILDING** | detail.

b. 1951 Santiago Calatrava

skeleton that was now no longer covered in cladding, but offered extensively glass-fronted façades. The Seagram Building is among the first of this generation (figs. left and above). Ludwig Mies van der Rohe (1886–1969) designed it in collaboration with Philip Johnson (1906–2005). Mies was convinced that the structural skeleton of a building should not be completely covered up, but should remain visible. As he argued in the magazine *Frühlicht* in 1922: "Skyscrapers reveal their bold structural pattern during construction. Only then does the gigantic steel web seem impressive. When the outer walls are put in place, the structural system which is the basis of all artistic design is hidden by a chaos of meaningless and trivial forms. When finished, these buildings are impressive only because of their size; yet they should surely be more than mere examples of our technical ability...." In the Seagram Building he put these ideas into practice. The highrise office building, erected in 1958 on New York's Park Avenue, is a rectangle 157

meters high with a glass "curtain wall." From the outside the bronze-colored lines of the steel skeleton are visible. This horizontal articulation is only absent from the topmost stories: these are the service areas of the skyscraper, not offices, and thus their function is also legible from the outside.

Skyscrapers are an American art form, although they have existed around the globe for a long time as residential or office spaces, housing department stores, restaurants, or theaters, etc. The most recent highrise record has been logged by the United Arab Emirates: in 2004 Dubai saw the beginning of an attempt to beat the height record. The Burj Khalifa, which opened in 2010, succeeded: at 830 meters it is the highest building ever, clearly beating the previous frontrunner in Taiwan, the 509-meter-high office block Taipei 101. Dubai's Burj Khalifa consists of three buttresses on a Y-shaped plan: the reinforced concrete buttresses support each other and can thus withstand torsion despite their enormous height. The tower's façades are built of different layers: on the coast-facing side they shelter the tower against strong sunlight; on the land-facing side they offer protection against the hot desert wind. Apartments, offices, and a hotel are accommodated in over 160 stories, all made of steel, concrete, and glass (fig. pp. 122/123). Why do we still want to build skyscrapers? Why build them at all? In the end it is certainly not

left—LUDWIG MIES VAN DER ROHE, SEAGRAM BUILDING | New York 1955.
above left—LUDWIG MIES VAN DER ROHE, SEAGRAM BUILDING entrance area.
above right—LUDWIG MIES VAN DER ROHE, SEAGRAM BUILDING | detail.

1989—Fall of the Berlin Wall .... **2008**—Beginning of the Global Financial Crisis··· SKYSCRAPERS **122/123**

.... **2001**—Terrorist attacks on World Trade Center ('9/11') ....

.... **2002**—Introduction of the Euro ....

"The Burj Khalifa with its 830 meters is the highest building ever."

always lack of space which is responsible for the drive upwards. Philip Johnson, himself an architect of several highrise buildings, had his own opinions on the matter: "What is there about the desire for domination, or to reach God, or for private pride—the Pyramids are an example of that, but the tall building is certainly another. Every civilization is touched by that desire—the Aztecs with their great stairs, the pagodas in China, the temples in Southern India, the Gothic cathedrals like Ulm. They all reached for a dominant height." And what

about the kind of skyscrapers he himself built? "In the commercial world, the skyscraper came into existence because we didn't have any religion to express. But it was an expression, not the result of economic needs. It was an expression that wanted to reach the heavens—whether Mr. Rockefeller at Rockefeller Center or the Chicago architects, for instance, who weren't interested so much in the steel skeletons people are always writing books about. It was an attempt to go up.... " And clearly this has by no means disappeared.

left—ADRIAN SMITH OF SKIDMORE, OWINGS AND MERRILL, BURJ KHALIFA | Dubai | 2010.

next double page spread—VIEW OF TAIPEI WITH TAIPEI FINANCIAL CENTER BY C. Y. LEE & PARTNERS | 1999–2004.

1806—Battle of Trafalgar ·· **1861–1865**—American Civil War ··· **126/127**

··· **1853–1856**—Crimean War ···

1803–1865 Joseph Paxton   1832–1923 Gustave Eiffel

THE FIRST HOUSES MADE OF GLASS

The first houses which used glass in a big way were created for plants: orangeries, which helped delicate citrus trees from the South to flourish in cooler regions, appeared in many parks and gardens in northern Europe in the eighteenth century. These greenhouses were supported by iron structures so that their walls could be made of glass. Thus a protective shell for delicate plants was created, which at the same time served their need for daylight.

At this time two developments in material technology gave glass architecture an important upturn: firstly the new building material of iron meant that stone masonry could be dispensed with; and secondly large-scale production of glass gained momentum around 1830 and provided supplies in large quantities. However this was not the first great moment for glass in architecture, as highly colored glass windows had already played a leading role in Gothic cathedrals. But only now and with the aid of iron architecture could traditional ideas of space be transcended: what was previously a stone mass was now replaced by a metal structure of economical dimensions completed by glass as an external skin. Transparent spaces emerged which were soon valued

as more than just garden architecture. Shopping arcades and railway station halls—both building types which only emerged during the period of industrialization—profited from the combination of iron and glass. And glass played a large role in exhibition buildings as well: a prototype of iron-and-glass architecture was created with London's Crystal Palace, which housed the first World's Fair in 1851 (see also pp. 102–105).

Building with glass was also a major theme among the architectural avant-garde of the early 1920s. By opposing the solidly built house with the house of glass, it was intended that light should enter architecture, and in the metaphorical sense it suffused civilization as well. The glass exhibition pavilion by Bruno Taut (1880–1938) that was created for the German Werkbund Exhibition of 1914 in Cologne is an example of this. Glass art and the glass industry were to be represented at the exhibition as an important economic element in the German Reich through many pavilions. One pavilion was designed by Taut himself: his exhibition building was a glazed house and thus, according to its creator "has no function other than to be beautiful" (Taut's pamphlet for visitors to the Glass Pavilion, 1914). Beneath a dome of multicolored glass Taut's design stood on a polygonal ground-plan. Only the base was made of concrete and above this rose a circumference of glass

left—**BRUNO TAUT, EXTERIOR VIEW OF THE GLASS PAVILION** | Cologne 1914.

128/129 GLASS ARCHITECTURE ······· **1873**—Jules Verne publishes *Around the World in Eighty Days* ·················· **1933**—Adolf Hitler seizes power

1876—Battle of the Little Bighorn ··············· **1884**—Mark Twain publishes the *Adventures of Huckleberry Finn* ···························

1883—Friedrich Nietzsche publishes *Thus Spoke Zarathustra* ···························

1883–1969 Walter Gropius   1906–2005 Philip Johnson

"With the house of glass, it was intended that light should suffuse civilization in the metaphorical sense as well."

plates. Inside, a glass staircase led up into the space under the dome, in which manufactured glass objects were exhibited, and whose floor was also made of glass prisms. The building only lasted for four weeks as the exhibition was closed early in August 1914 when war broke out. However the architectural vision behind the Glass Pavilion has lasted for decades. "Brick will ever pass away/Where tinted glass will thrive and stay" read one of the aphorisms by poet Paul Sheerbart in his celebration of glass architecture, writing these words on the walls of Taut's Pavilion itself.

Glass has also continued to thrive in terms of architectural history as glass architecture has remained an issue for the Modernist architects. In industrial architecture, Walter Gropius (1883–1969) and Adolf Meyer (1881–1929) distinguished themselves with a building that gave glass a central role. The Fagus shoe-last factory in Alfeld in Lower Saxony, Germany, was built between 1911 and 1913 and is one of the founding buildings of modern architecture. The office building is a three-story, elongated rectangle in which the floors and stairwells seem to be suspended from invisible points. But the building stands out even today because of its structurally ingenious steel-and-glass façade, which forms a curtain of glass. Many non-load-bearing elements of the building are made of glass, and even the building's corners are completely glazed (fig. left). Residential building was not left untouched by this development. In Paris Pierre Chareau (1883–1950) created a private house from glass bricks (fig. p. 130). The entire courtyard façade of the Maison de Verre (completed in 1932) is built from glass bricks, which

left—**WALTER GROPIUS AND ADOLF MEYER, FAGUS FACTORY** | Alfeld 1911–13.

above—**PHILIP JOHNSON, GLASS HOUSE** | Connecticut | 1947–49.

130/131 GLASS ARCHITECTURE ············ **1939–1945**—Second World War ·· **1992**—Founding of the European Union
·· **1969**—Neil Armstrong lands on the moon ····················
··· **1989**—Fall of the Berlin Wall ····················

are fitted into a metal framework and filter daylight. Chareau continued his use of glass in the interior, where moveable glass partitions provide a flexible division of space. Glass residences also emerged in the United States. "The Glass House is really a series of frames that define the views of nearby trees and lawns...." (Peter Blake, *Philip Johnson*, Birkhäuser Verlag/Basel 1996) Thus architecture critic Peter Blake described the home of American architect Philip Johnson (1906–2005), one of the most famous Modernist buildings (fig. p. 129). Fundamentally, then, the Glass House is no longer a house. The glass rectangular block sits on a wide area of lawn, blending in completely with its surroundings. Inside, a brick structure, which stands slightly proud above the flat roof of the building, is the only non-glass element in the house. Apart from this structure the symmetrical building is only discernible by means of its steel frame, in particular the massive corner

supports of the dark gray framework which Johnson emphasized. Everything else is glass. The glass Modernist houses, with their 360-degree view of space, perpetuate a Gothic idea: the coming together of light and space.

In the last few decades glass architects and engineers have developed the constructive potential of the material even further. Thanks to improvements in the materials, glass has become applicable to an ever-increasing number of uses. Glass curtain walls, such as those installed by Gropius and Meyer for the first time in the Fagus Factory, had quickly become established, particularly for skyscrapers, in the second half of the twentieth century. Even away from highrise building, glass architecture is never at a loss for spectacular projects. For example, the glass dome for the Reichstag in Berlin by Norman Foster (b. 1935), which was completed in 1999, demonstrates the structural development of building with glass (fig. right).

above—PIERRE CHAREAU, MAISON DE VERRE | Paris | 1928–32.
right—NORMAN FOSTER, DOME OF THE REICHSTAG | Berlin | 1994–99.
next double page spread—HELMUT JAHN, SONY CENTER | Berlin 1996–2000 | detail of the glass roof.

1900—Sigmund Freud publishes *The Interpretation of Dreams* ··· **1905**—Formation of the expressionist group Die Brücke···

1900—Beginning of the Boxer Rebellion in China ······························· **1903**—First powered flight by the Wright brothers ··

134/135

FIRST FUNCTION, THEN FORM

At the beginning of the twentieth century, the notion that architectural form can develop from the inner function of a building increased in popularity. After the architects of the previous century had reveled in the architectural styles of history, repeatedly quoting past eras, the style of a building was now considered of secondary importance. Many architects found it more interesting to ask how one could give priority to the *purpose* of a building. No historicizing decoration should adorn the façades—in modern buildings it was a question of letting function express itself and be recognizable structurally on the exterior of the building. Glass, steel, and concrete constructions appeared, in which the building's requirements for use were afforded the highest priority. At the same time, after World War I this new orientation towards functionalism also acquired a social component. In their modern designs architects were not only trying to capture the zeitgeist, but they also wanted to develop rational, cheap, and quick building methods to combat the acute housing shortage.

The prototype of functionalist architecture—and of the clear modernization of the arts in general—was the Bauhaus. The connection between art and craft was of prime importance in the creative process at the Bauhaus school, which architect Walter Gropius (1883–1969) took over as director in 1919. This connection was to be achieved in all areas of art: in the Bauhaus workshops, masters and students devoted themselves to painting and photography, industrial design and architecture, dance and theater. Different artistic personalities, including Theo van Doesburg (1883–1931), Oskar Schlemmer (1888–1934), and Wassily Kandinsky (1866–1944), worked at the Bauhaus until the school was closed in 1932 at the instigation of the Nazis. Even before this, the political pressure on the avant-garde art school had been enormous, so much so that in 1925 the Bauhaus in Weimar had to close and open again in Dessau. Architecturally this new beginning was the creation of Walter Gropius: "It is an auspicious prelude that the Bauhaus is allowed to erect its own casing," he commented; and he completed the building, which was to unite all the arts and crafts activities under one roof, in just thirteen months.

"Architecture should be a mirror of our life and times, and so we must recognize in its contemporary features the leading forces of our era." This was

left—**WALTER GROPIUS WITH ADOLF MEYER, BAUHAUS** | Dessau 1925/26 | staircase.

1906—San Francisco earthquake .... **1911**—Roald Amundsen reaches the South Pole ....
....**1909**—Opening of Queensboro Bridge in New York ....
....**1914 – 1918**—First World War ....

b. 1907 Oscar Niemeyer   1910 – 1961 Eero Saarinen

Gropius's motto as an architect. And the school's new building turned out to be correspondingly modern too. In Dessau three L-shaped wings were built, combining to form an asymmetric site (figs. above and right). Gropius rigorously separated the different functions of the building—such as studios, living quarters, and administration—and allocated them to the different wings of the building. In turn the content of each wing could be "read" from the façade as a result of these structural differences. The most spectacular of the three parts of the building, in visual terms, was the workshop wing. Here the work and exhibition spaces for the different departments in the school were housed over four floors. On the side facing the street, the entire wing was glass-fronted, thus creating optimal light conditions in the studios. Even the wings housing the library and administration, and the students' living quarters, enjoyed a large amount of window space. Here, by contrast with the workshop wing, wide strip windows made the separation of the stories legible. All the school's arts and crafts disciplines worked hand-in-hand to create an institution in Dessau that was to become the epitome of modern architecture.

above and right—**BAUHAUS** | Dessau.

1913 – 2005 Kenzo Tange   **b. 1917 Ieoh Ming Pei**

1919—Founding of the Weimar Republic ···································· **1922**—Discovery of Tutankhamun's Tomb ···············
·· **1919**—Formation of the Bauhaus school·································

1918–2008 Jørn Utzon   **1922–2010 Günter Behnisch**

According to the school's manifesto, artists, architects, sculptors, and painters should ultimately be able to work towards "the new building of the future." Appropriately, the in-house mural painting department took on the job of decorating the walls of the new building; the students in the metal workshops designed lamps and tubular steel furniture; and the Bauhaus print department created the logos. Soon "Bauhaus" was no longer just the perfect example of an art school, but it also epitomized the style Gropius had founded. Its aim was to determine an aesthetic, with materials-based construction determining creative expression. In retrospect, the Bauhaus student, Max Bill (1908–94), described this process, writing in lower case letters as was customary at the Bauhaus: "functionalism originally arose under the pretext of locating function as either the basis or the justification for design decisions." (Max Bill, 'From Functionalism to Function' (1979) in *Form, Function, Beauty = Gestalt*, London: The Architectural Association, 2010)
The Bauhaus architects' "design decisions" inclined towards cuboid architectural structures, clear white surfaces, and symmetrical rows of windows. This approach was to cause a worldwide sensation. The central credo of architectural modernity, "form follows function," can be attributed to Louis Sullivan (1856–1924). However, the American architect

and theorist was not demanding the rejection of ornament, but rather that architectural decoration should be in keeping with the building itself. The new architecture of the 1920s, by contrast, presented itself as more radical, and rejected any architectural ornamentation. The "New Building" as advocated by Walter Gropius consisted of white cubes with flat roofs.
The industrialization of house building was also an important topic in this context. Attempts by the Art Nouveau movement to oppose industrial mass production had come to nothing, so now it was time to take advantage of its benefits. Gropius, for example, envisaged the mechanization of architectural production: he believed that the mass production of houses would become possible through the standardization of architectural components. At the Deutscher Werkbund exhibition in Stuttgart in 1927, Gropius presented new solutions for construction using prefabrication. Gropius was one

above left—Mies van der Rohe, experimental housing, Weissenhof | Stuttgart | 1927.
above right—Experimental housing, Weissenhof rear of Houses 3/4.
right—Experimental housing, Weissenhof | apartment house.

1925—Invention of television .... FUNCTIONALISM **138/139**

b. 1925 Frei Otto   b. 1929 Frank O. Gehry

1931—Completion of the Empire State Building .... **1933**—Adolf Hitler seizes power ....

b. 1932 Peter Eisenman   b. 1933 Richard Rogers   b. 1935 Norman Foster

of sixteen avant-garde architects showing their built designs for contemporary living. On a site above Stuttgart called Weissenhof, they presented their highly contemporary housing estate under the artistic direction of Ludwig Mies van der Rohe (1886–1969) (figs. p. 138 and 139). Alongside Gropius and Mies van der Rohe other participating architects included Peter Behrens (1868–1940) and Le Corbusier (1887–1965). Despite their different backgrounds and architectural opinions, the numerous participants were agreed on the question of form and use of materials: for them the homes of the future meant simple, cube-like structures with white façades, a flat roof, large windows, and the visible use of metal. The movement that focused on "New Building" was international. As an "International Style," which was celebrated for its cube buildings with glass and steel façades, the movement's approach shaped the face of cities until long after World War II.

With its demand that internal organizational structures should determine the form of a building's exterior, functionalism as an international architectural language had correspondingly many variations. Finnish architect Alvar Aalto (1898–1976) pursued an influential course, which combined the ideas of functional building with the architectural traditions of his native land. Aalto included the landscape surrounding a building at the heart of the creative process, placing great value on wood, which was and is frequently used in Finnish architecture, in his designs for both houses and furniture. Aalto combined these characteristics with the criteria of functional building. As a result of this combination, his sanatorium in Paimio in southern Finland became an icon of modern architecture (figs. above and right). Aalto finished work on the building in 1933: he had created his first great work of architecture, a tuberculosis clinic in the space of five years, in the middle of a forest. The building's various wings in whitewashed concrete with flat roofs stretch

b. 1937 Renzo Piano

*"The architecture of Alvar Aalto,
interior as well as exterior,
was to have the most positive impact
possible on the residents."*

away into the forest. They are structured differently according to their different functions. But above all light, air, and sun were to be the determining factors in the building complex, and this also corresponded to the requirements of tuberculosis treatment of that time. Aalto's design for a ward block was an innovation in hospital architecture. The narrow building contains numerous rooms for the patients; the architect succeeded in making every one of them south-facing, providing them with as much daylight as possible. The administration block lies to the north of the site, as far away as possible from the patients' rooms in order to avoid any disruption of the necessary peace and quiet.

Aalto's approach was "to make architecture more human." In Paimio, for example, he included in his planning of the patients' rooms the idea that they are created for people who are lying down, and he adapted the arrangement of the windows and doors, as well as color scheme, lighting, and heating of the rooms, to this situation. Aalto even designed most of the furniture himself, using primarily wood, which he preferred to metal. His Paimio chair made of birch wood is anatomically adapted to the needs of the patient, and remains one of the most famous and sought-after pieces of Aalto furniture to this day. The architecture, interior as well as exterior, was to have the most positive impact possible on the residents, and for Aalto functionalist building certainly did not exclude this: "An architectural solution must always have a human motive based on analysis, but that motive has to be materialized in construction that probably is a result of extraneous circumstances." ("The Humanizing of Architecture" in *Alvar Aalto: Sketches*, edited by Göran Schildt, trans. Stuart Wrede, MIT Press, 1978, p. 79)

left—ALVAR AALTO, SANATORIUM | Paimio | 1929–33.
above—VIEW FROM THE NORTHWEST OF THE SANATORIUM WARD BLOCK.

1883—First petrol-engined automobile .... 1896—First modern Olympic Games ....
1886—Completion of the Statue of Liberty ....
1889—Completion of the Eiffel Tower ....

142/143

1883–1969 Walter Gropius   1886–1969 Ludwig Mies van der Rohe   1898–1976 Alvar Aalto

BUILDING WITH LIGHT

The transformation of night into day is a quite recent phenomenon. The nighttime cityscape only changed at the end of the nineteenth century through electrification, simultaneously causing life to extend further and further into the evening hours. Streetlights turned night into daylight on the streets where passersby could wander past illuminated shop windows. Thanks to artificial lighting, building façades displayed effects of light and shadow which could not be seen during the day. Finally, even interiors were illuminated: electric lighting was first employed in 1880 in the large London railway stations. Electricity was particularly important at the Paris World's Fair. In 1889 the Eiffel Tower was already displaying a variety of lighting methods created by architect Gustave Eiffel (1832–1923), and electricity was shown in all its facets in its own Palais d'Électricité in 1900.

Outlining the contours of a building with electric light bulbs or floodlighting it dramatically was, however, only the first step. Hard on the heels of architectural illumination came the first ideas about building with light and about nocturnal architecture. This was of interest to Ludwig Mies van der Rohe (1886–1969), whose German Pavilion at the World's Fair in Barcelona in 1929 was a first in the architecture of light. A lavish light concept was created for the entire Fair: adjoining the pavilions, flights of steps and fountains in the gardens were incorporated into the design, becoming all-night stars of a spectacular light show. Mies's Barcelona Pavilion also opted for lighting effects, albeit in a reduced way. The architecture is simple and limited to walls made of glass and stone with a flat roof supported by free-standing columns. The architectural forms are reflected in two pools, and this creates a connection between interior and exterior space. Between the space under the roof and the terrace, the architect placed a double wall of frosted glass. At night this intermediate space was illuminated by interior lights which provided an indirect form of lighting. The double wall shed a white light in both directions. In terms of his lighting effects, Mies's design referred back to the lighting idea of an earlier World's Fair architect. Bruno Taut, who had built a glass pavilion for the German Werkbund Exhibition of 1914 in Cologne, also included nocturnal effects in his design from the start (see also pp. 126/127). Glass as a building material gave Taut direct access to the

left—PEI COBB FREED & PARTNERS, BANK OF AMERICA TOWER
Miami | 1983–87.

.... **1914–1918**—First World War .... **1939–1945**—Second World War ....
.... **1919**—Founding of the Weimar Republic ....
.... **1922**—Discovery of Tutankhamun's Tomb ....

1922–2010 Günter Behnisch   **b. 1937 Rafael Moneo**

element of light: "In a glass house one has no need of electric light bulbs and suchlike for 'illumination'," wrote Taut in 1914. "One only has to provide the rooms of the glass house with light and from the outside it will seem most beautifully illuminated." Architects certainly did not lose interest in electrical light as a design element even in the second half of the twentieth century. The architect of the Pirelli Tower in Milan, Gio Ponti (1891–1979), worked with "architecture of the night," as he called it. He wrote in 1957 that he always designed two forms of architecture, one for day and one for night: "Lighting will become a central factor in the architecture of space.... We will create a new city of the night." Several designs from recent times seem to endorse Ponti's view. In San Sebastián on the Atlantic coast of Spain, architect Rafael Moneo (b. 1937) created a convention center, which since 1999 has presented

different faces to the harbor town depending on the time of day, and produces a spectacular night-time effect (fig. p. 145). During the day the two main structures in the center, the Chamber Hall and the Auditorium, simply display their glass façades, which enclose the structures in horizontal strips. At night the Chamber Hall and Auditorium are transformed into radiant squares filled with multi-colored light. Recently the Swiss architectural duo

above left—**GEORGE GAREN, BURNING EIFFEL TOWER** | color etching Paris, Musée d'Orsay.
above right—**LUDWIG MIES VAN DER ROHE, GERMAN PAVILION AT THE WORLD'S FAIR IN BARCELONA** | 1929.
right—**RAFAEL MONEO, KURSAAL: THE AUDITORIUM AND CHAMBER HALL** | San Sebastián | 1990–99.

1949—Founding of the Federal Republic of Germany ························· **1961**—Construction of the Berlin Wall··········· **1969**—Neil Armstrong lands on the moon··· **LIGHT** 144/145

1968—Assassination of Martin Luther King ··

b. 1945 Jean Nouvel   b. 1951 Santiago Calatrava

146/147 LIGHT .... **1989**—Fall of the Berlin Wall.. **2011**—Arab Spring.......................
2001—Terrorist attacks on World Trade Center ('9/11')....................
2002—Introduction of the Euro...............................

"4,500 LEDs on the façade of the building enable the Torre Agbar in Barcelona to shimmer in sixteen million colors."

Herzog & de Meuron (both b. 1950) have designed a soccer stadium with a nocturnal effect. The Allianz Arena in Munich, Germany, which opened in 2005, is clad with a membrane made of almost 3,000 air-filled panels. This synthetic wall can change color: each of the translucent panels can be lit separately, according to which team is playing, in red, blue, or white, or even a combination. And in Barcelona a round office tower has been lit up since 2005. Architect Jean Nouvel (b. 1945) created the Torre Agbar: the over-140-meter-high glass tower is the headquarters of the city's water company,

Aguas de Barcelona, which also gave its name to the tower. Nouvel counts light in all its forms and qualities among his obsessions. In fact the 16,000-square-meter façade of the thirty-five stories appears colored even during the day, but it shines only at night. Light artist Yann Kersalé created the light installation: each of the 4,500 LEDs on the façade of the building can be switched on separately, glowing blue, red, pink, or yellow. Even color transitions can be achieved independently from one another, thus enabling Barcelona's highrise tower to shimmer in sixteen million colors (fig. right).

right—JEAN NOUVEL, TORRE AGBAR | Barcelona | 2005.
next double page spread—PAUL ANDREU, NATIONAL CENTER FOR THE PERFORMING ARTS ('THE EGG') | Beijing | 2001–08.

1900—Beginning of the Boxer Rebellion in China
1903—First powered flight by the Wright brothers
1906—San Francisco earthquake
1909—Opening of Queensboro Bridge in New York

150/151

1906–2005 Philip Johnson b. 1907 Oscar Niemeyer   1910–1961 Eero Saarinen

RAW AND UNADORNED: THE FIRST REINFORCED CONCRETE BUILDINGS

Concrete is by no means a twentieth-century invention, but it was only then that the material came to play a leading role in architecture. Concrete was already used in Antiquity: the Romans used this artificial stone to build the Pantheon, for example. Concrete is a mixture of mortar and stones, with mortar itself being made of water, sand, and cement. This mixture is poured into a mold and then hardens into a pressure- and water-resistant material. In the case of the Pantheon in Rome it was concrete that ensured that the 43-meter-wide dome could exist without any form of support (see also pp. 30–32). By comparison with stone the material is relatively light and, moreover, offers a wider range of shapes than the more brittle material of wood.

After the masterly achievement of the Pantheon in Antiquity, concrete returned to prominence only in the nineteenth century. And then metal was added to concrete. Liquid concrete is poured into a mold in which there are steel rods or a steel framework; the concrete completely encloses these steel components, thus combining both materials to form reinforced concrete. In this hybrid construction of

stone and iron, the steel absorbs the tensile forces and the artificial stone of concrete absorbs the load forces.

At the beginning of the twentieth century, the first building to use this new material was constructed in the United States. The Ingalls Building in Cincinnati is supported by a skeleton of steel-reinforced concrete. However, this cannot be seen from the exterior, as the façade of the sixteen-story building was completely clad in stone. In the process of construction itself the material played an important role. Leaving the reinforced concrete framework of a building visible was still unpopular at this time. Around the turn of the century, Belgian Auguste Perret (1874–1954) began to employ reinforced concrete and used the still-new material over the following decades for numerous building projects, including spectacular church designs using exposed concrete. The architect also worked on residential projects, and had recourse to reinforced concrete in these instances. In 1903 Perret built a multistory apartment and commercial building on the Rue Franklin in Paris in which the concrete framework was deliberately left unconcealed, or rather the load-bearing construction can be read on the façade as a grid of horizontal and vertical stripes. Between the concrete the architect still left space for ornamentation using vegetal motifs. Large windows are inser-

left—LE CORBUSIER, CORBUSIERHAUS | Berlin Charlottenburg | 1956–58.

152/153 CONCRETE ········· **1912**—Sinking of the Titanic ·· **1919**—Founding of the Weimar Republic
1914–1918—First World War ············· **1917**—October Revolution in Russia ···············

1913–2005 Kenzo Tange   1918–2008 Jørn Utzon   1922–2010 Günter Behnisch

ted into the concrete framework with its U-shaped gap.

Concrete houses increased in importance in the 1920s, and prototypes for entire housing developments emerged. At the Werkbund Exhibition in Stuttgart in 1927, for example, several houses made of reinforced concrete were exhibited, including designs by Walter Gropius, Ludwig Mies van der Rohe, and Le Corbusier. However, with the international economic crisis of 1929, experiments in the industrialization of residential building in Germany came to a temporary end.

Around the middle of the century, concrete became *the* Modernist material. The leader of the movement focusing on *béton brut*, or raw concrete, was the architect, city planner, and theorist Le Corbusier (1887–1965). Throughout his life Swiss-born Le Corbusier pursued the idea of mass-producing houses and the radical new planning of entire cities in concrete. In the Unité d'Habitation, which was built on the outskirts of Marseille between 1953 and 1955, Le Corbusier turned his ideas about collective living into reality—and into concrete (fig. above). A reinforced-concrete framework supports the 165-meter-long apartment block, which is supported by massive pillars. The building makes no secret of its material: concrete, still bearing the imprints of the mold into which it was poured, characterizes both the interiors and the exterior, accentuated by the addition of color. The 18-story "machine for living" proclaims its self-sufficiency as the architect presents it as the union of dwelling and living. Alongside over 330 duplex apartments, the Unité comprises stores, a hotel with restaurant, a school, kindergarten, and swimming pool. This Marseille building was intended to be a prototype for further

above—**Le Corbusier, Unité d'Habitation** | Marseille.
right—**Auguste Perret, Apartment Building** | Rue Franklin | Paris.

154/155 CONCRETE ········· 1925—Invention of television·· 1933—Adolf Hitler seizes power

1931—Completion of the Empire State Building··················

apartment buildings, and some were even built. An emphasis on the raw concrete structure, uncleaned and unclad, was the hallmark of building with *béton brut*. Like Perret before him, Le Corbusier also applied this form to church building. His design for the pilgrimage chapel at Ronchamp greatly influenced church building in the second half of the twentieth century. The architect even created a monastery out of exposed concrete: from 1953 to 1960 he worked on the site of Sainte Marie de La Tourette (fig. above). Le Corbusier created the monastery for the mendicant order of Dominicans using a framework of reinforced concrete. The rectangular-plan building appears as a block in an open landscape, its unplastered façades revealing the individual concrete parts. Three wings arranged in a U-shape, which house the monastery, create the rectangular ground-plan, alongside a fourth wing, somewhat detached, which constitutes the church. The latter is an unstructured box which is only recognizable as a church from the outside by

its bell-tower, and which is lit by narrow openings and strip windows.

The use of reinforced concrete should not be equated with an abandonment of light, filigree structures, and this is made clear above all in the buildings of the Brazilian architect Oscar Niemeyer (b. 1907). The lightness of many of his designs has in the first instance nothing in common with the heavy material of reinforced concrete. With Niemeyer's designs for Pampulha reinforced concrete entered a new era: until then the material had been used in the rigid form prescribed by its metal structure. Niemeyer changed that: "I introduced the curve as a form for architecture. For me the curve was the natural form

above—LE CORBUSIER, SAINTE MARIE DE LA TOURETTE | Éveux sur L'Arbresle | 1952–60.

right—DENYS LASDUN, ROYAL NATIONAL THEATRE | London | 1967–76.

for concrete." In Belo Horizonte, north of Rio de Janeiro towards the interior of Brazil, Niemeyer designed the center of a new district, Pampulha, on the banks of a man-made lake. The sculptural possibilities offered by reinforced concrete were exploited by the architect in his designs. In 1940 he used concrete in wave-like forms which are clad with colored tiles and which follow the curved edge of the lake for the roof of the colonnade at the Casa do Baile in Pampulha (fig. left). Niemeyer also employed undulations in reinforced concrete in his designs for Brasília. The new capital city was founded between 1957 and 1960 and was intended to express Brazil's rise as an industrialized nation. This concrete planned city, developed to a great extent by urban planner Lúcio Costa (1902–1998), appeared in the thinly populated interior of Brazil, at the geographical center of the country. As a result, Costa was bound neither to an already developed site nor to already existing buildings, and so could create buildings which suited this uncharted territory. Oscar Niemeyer located his governmental and cultural buildings along the six-kilometer north–south axis which runs through the city. Alongside ministries and the university are the Supreme Court and the Presidential Palace. Then there is the National Congress Building. Behind a flat building which houses the Chamber of Deputies and the Senate stands the highrise tower with the deputies' offices. Straight lines and right angles characterize the image, and the façades are broken up by glass.

left—OSCAR NIEMEYER, CASA DO BAILE | Pampulha, Brazil.
above—OSCAR NIEMEYER, NATIONAL CONGRESS BUILDING | Brasília, Brazil.

1948—Founding of the State of Israel
1959—Completion of the Solomon R. Guggenheim Museum
1949—Founding of the Federal Republic of Germany

b. 1951 Santiago Calatrava

But even here the curve is given a prominent role. A fundamental theme in Niemeyer's design was the optical emphasis on the two parliamentary chambers. Thus two bowl shapes sit in the middle of the flat roof: the dome of the Senate rises up hemispherically out of the roof, while the other bowl shape, turned upside down and thus open to the sky, is located above the Chamber of Deputies (fig. p. 157). Building with exposed concrete proceeded in different directions in the second half of the twentieth century. In Japan architect Kenzo Tange (1913–2005) used the material for many building projects. Designs such as the Yamanashi Press and Broadcasting Center in the Japanese city of Yamanashi emerged as real concrete castles in the Brutalist style (fig. above). Sixteen massive columns each five meters in diameter support the supply areas of the building, and between them are floors with office and studio spaces. Exposed concrete was employed not only for offices and industrial sites: in residential building, too, the material found a use in the second half of the twentieth century. Many residential projects of the 1960s show that modular building reached a creative dead-end and damaged the reputation of concrete as a revolutionary building material.

above—KENZO TANGE, YAMANASHI PRESS AND BROADCASTING CENTER | Kofu, Japan | 1961–66.
right—SANTIAGO CALATRAVA, AUDITORIO DE TENERIFE | Santa Cruz de Tenerife | finished 2003.

1961—Construction of the Berlin Wall ·· **1969**—Neil Armstrong lands on the moon··· **CONCRETE** **158/159**

1968—Assassination of Martin Luther King··

"The use of reinforced concrete should not be equated with an abandonment of light, filigree structures."

A MOMENTOUS INVENTION: ARCHISCULPTURE

Many thousands of years ago, architects focused on the results of the connection between architecture and sculpture. Ancient temples were decorated with sculptural ornamentation and later even the façades of medieval churches boasted sculptural designs, which had been elaborated in detail. But while the boundaries between the genres were still clearly drawn well into the twentieth century, in Modernist architecture they were beginning to blur. Architects started to give shape to their buildings as sculptors had done with their sculptures. For example, Erich Mendelsohn (1887–1953) built an astronomical observatory by modelling a structure in an organic way (fig. left). Even the project sketches, created with just a few dynamic lines, demonstrate his entirely individual approach (fig. below). The Tower, which is located in Potsdam just outside Berlin, was

intended to conduct research into Albert Einstein's theory of relativity, and so is called the Einstein Tower. A laboratory was set up in the base of the building, while in the dome complicated equipment enabled the observation of the sun and the skies. Research in the Einstein Tower began in 1924. Years after the observatory opened the German press commented, "In their early enthusiasm for his theory of relativity Einstein's friends have erected a peculiar observation tower." (*Die Wochenpost*, September, 1930) The shape of the building is certainly peculiar, its anthopomorphic tower resembling a helmeted knight in armor. One might also read the Einstein Tower as a white rough-cast sculpture constructed in concave and convex surfaces, as the sculptural expression of dynamically flowing forms.

left—Erich Mendelsohn, Einstein Tower | Potsdam | 1919–21.
right—Erich Mendelsohn, Sketch for Einstein Tower.

1919—Formation of the Bauhaus school ·········· 1922—Discovery of Tutankhamun's Tomb ·········· 1925—Invention of television ··········

1922–2010 Günter Behnisch   b. 1925 Frei Otto

"After World War II many architects began to focus on the sculptural nature of their designs – concrete became their preferred material."

While the Bauhaus architects made an impression with simple cuboid forms symmetrically arranged, and with wide façades of horizontal strip windows, the first signs of an architecture which was sculpturally expressive, like Mendelsohn's Einstein Tower, fell on fertile ground. After World War II some architects began to focus on the sculptural nature of their designs. Concrete was the preferred material of the proponents of this sculptural style. Mendelsohn had originally planned to use precast concrete for his Einstein Tower, but for structural reasons it was built in brick and covered in stucco. Le Corbusier (1887–1965) took full advantage of the sculptural possibilities that concrete had to offer. In his pilgrimage chapel at Ronchamp in the Vosges region of France, this champion of concrete created a building shaped by sculptural ideas (fig. right). Here Le Corbusier completely dispensed with right angles, straight sides, or symmetrical façades. The chapel, which was built between 1950 and 1954, presents an architectural sculpture in the middle of a green, softly undulating landscape on the top of a hill. The building is a windowless tower made of exposed concrete with a white, roughcast wall curved towards the south and pierced, apparently arbitrarily, by several window openings of different sizes. It is finished by a dark, heavy roof that bulges out beyond the façade. Only on the pointed southeast corner does the wall come to an end in a high pinnacle, like the bow of a ship, which keeps the projection of the roof in check. Le Corbusier's sculptural architecture for Ronchamp did not attract supporters in the same way that Mendelsohn's Einstein Tower had struggled to gain acceptance. The local press even described Ronchamp as an "ecclesiastical garage" or a "bedroom slipper."

His design was described as looking like "a Danish pastry": this was the uncomplimentary comparison that an architect had to put up with on the other side of the world. With his opera house in Sydney, Australia, Danish architect Jørn Utzon (1918–2008) had also ventured into the area of sculptural architecture. But it was not only in the area of contemporary taste that this design represented a risk: technically, too, it reached the limits of what was possible.

The building that today is the symbol of the city took shape between 1959 and 1973 on a small spit of land in Sydney Harbour. And what a building it is: like billowing sails, twelve white, up to sixty-meter-high concrete shells stand on a podium of natural stone. The structure is located on a plateau which affords an overview of the harbor and coast. The opera house

right—LE CORBUSIER, NOTRE DAME DU HAUT | Ronchamp | 1950–54.

b. 1929 Frank O. Gehry

b. 1933 Richard Rogers

1939 – 1945—Second World War ·· **1941**—Pearl Harbor attack ································

b. 1937 Rafael Moneo   b. 1944 Bernard Tschumi

"On a small spit of land in Sydney Harbour, twelve white concrete shells stand on a podium of natural stone."

b. 1945 Jean Nouvel   b. 1946 Daniel Libeskind   b. 1951 Santiago Calatrava

is surrounded on three sides by water, to which the architect refers in the sail-like forms of his roof outline. The undulating surfaces are clad with large, white-glazed ceramic tiles that reflect the sunlight. The shells have no direct function, but they characterize the sculptural effect of the building (fig. p. 164). They form the roof of the opera house itself which lies below them, as all facilities are housed in the lower podium structure. The opera house can seat 7,000 spectators, divided into two halls: one large one for symphony concerts, opera, or ballet; and a smaller one for theatrical performances or chamber concerts. The technical realization of the innovative shell structures, as well as the building's statics and acoustics, was the job of the studio of Anglo-Danish engineer Ove Arup (1895–1988). The task was not easy, as the engineer himself made clear, describing it in 1965 as "one of those not infrequent cases where the best architectural form and the best structural form are not the same." For Utzon the visual experience was of central importance: his opera house sculpture was even standing on a plinth and, like a sculpture in a museum, one could move around it.

left—JØRN UTZON, OPERA HOUSE SYDNEY | 1959–73.
above—JØRN UTZON, OPERA HOUSE SYDNEY | detail of the interior.

In Sydney, reactions to the building of the new opera house were mixed, not least because of the escalating building costs. Nevertheless, across the world, architectural concrete sculptures found their advocates. In New York, for example, curator Hilla Rebay asked for a "monument" when she placed her order for a museum building. The still fledgling collection of abstract painting which industralist Solomon Guggeheim had brought together needed a roof over its head. To the architect Frank Lloyd Wright (1869–1959), who was finally awarded the commission, she wrote: "I need a fighter, a lover of space, an agitator, a tester and a wise man." Wright, who at this time had long been the Modernist American architect par excellence, began work in 1943 on numerous designs for the new building, whose daring formal language found favor with both the collector and Hilla Rebay. The Guggenheim Museum on Central Park finally took shape between 1956 and 1959 (fig. pp. 166/167). Only then did they find a contractor, George Cohen, who was prepared to venture into architecturally uncharted territory alongside Wright. The museum that finally emerged on Fifth Avenue between 88th and 89th Streets, was far removed from architectural traditions. In the middle of Manhattan there arose a walk-in sculpture, which presented quite different aspects according to the direction the visitor approached it from.

1971—Completion of the Aswan Dam··· **ARCHISCULPTURE** 166/167
1968—Assassination of Martin Luther King
1969—Neil Armstrong lands on the moon

FRANK LLOYD WRIGHT, SOLOMON R. GUGGENHEIM MUSEUM
New York | 1956 – 59.

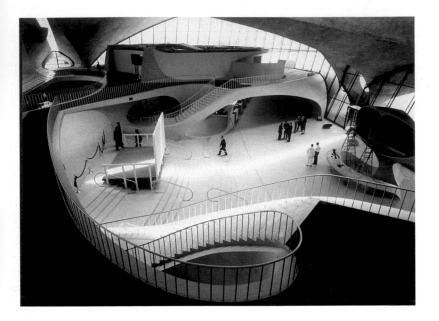

A stack of round disks, increasing in diameter towards the top, stands in splendor above a lower story. The interior space of the cone-like building is best experienced by the visitor from the top. The elevator takes one up to the top floor, above which light falls through a glass dome into the large central space. The museum can then be discovered on foot via a spiral ramp, which hugs the outside wall of the building. The ivory-colored Guggenheim building revived once again the controversy over sculptural architecture, as not all critics were convinced of the suitability of the structure as an art museum. Sculptural architecture can even be made to speak about its own impact, as Finnish architect Eero Saarinen (1910–61) proved. That a building should express its function was already a conviction among architects at the time of the French Revolution. In his design for the departure terminal building at New York's John F. Kennedy airport, Saarinen seems to have remembered this. Like the wings of a bird preparing to take flight, the terminal's roof spans the ocher-colored building (fig. above and right). Saarinen said clearly that, with his terminal design for what was then New York's largest airport, he wanted to capture nothing less than the "spirit of flight." For the expressively organic building, where the form already indicates the content, concrete was the ideal material. The TWA Flight Center, which was finished in 1962, is a construction in prestressed concrete supported by just a few Y-shaped pillars. The pillars continue the curved lines of the roof shell. Under the shallow vaulting of the concrete roof light streams into the interior of the terminal through large expanses of window. The curved forms persist in the interior too: everything in the 12,000-square-meter space, from roof to check-in desks and flight information displays, moves along curved lines. The architect of this unique architectural sculpture worked as a sculptor before transferring to architecture, which explains his acknowledged interest in sculptural forms.

above—EERO SAARINEN, TWA FLIGHT CENTER | New York | 1956–62
interior view
right—TWA FLIGHT CENTER | detail

1967—Six-Day War between Israel and neighboring Arab states⋯⋯⋯⋯⋯⋯⋯⋯⋯⋯⋯⋯⋯⋯⋯ **170/171**
1968—Assassination of Martin Luther King⋯⋯⋯⋯⋯⋯⋯⋯⋯⋯⋯⋯⋯⋯⋯⋯⋯⋯
1969—Neil Armstrong lands on the moon⋯⋯⋯⋯⋯⋯⋯⋯⋯⋯⋯⋯⋯⋯

THE TRIUMPH OF HIGH-TECH

The requirement of no longer leaving the construction of a building hidden from view but presenting it directly on a building's façade, emerged for the first time in the iron architecture of the nineteenth century. The high-tech architects of the 1970s took it a major step further: they explicitly laid great stress on the technical elements of their buildings, turning them inside-out, so to speak. They believed that industrial processes should determine the aesthetic of a building. The formal language of high-tech architecture is wholly derived from the possibilities of industrial technology. Public buildings and industrial buildings in particular demonstrate the range of this architectural trend. It encompasses modern technologies, the application of materials not normally used in architecture, or the overemphasis of construction details on the façade of a building. Today's high-tech designs are characterized above all by metal and glass: lightness of construction materials and their transparency, starting with glass façades, are typical. In this style the influence of engineers such as Frei Otto (b. 1925) and Ove Arup (1895–1988) is thus considerable, if the architect himself is not doubly talented as both architect and engineer, as in the case of Santiago Calatrava (b. 1951). By the 1950s, engineer Frei Otto was experimenting with lightweight, wide-span tensile structures for avant-garde cable-net constructions, which could cover large areas. His design for the Olympic Games in Munich in 1972 became a symbol of sporting achievement (fig. pp. 172/173). The Olympic Park was built between 1968 and 1972 on a three-square-kilometer site, where architect Günther Behnisch (1922–2010) decided against creating massive buildings. The park landscape in the north of the city matched the commissioners' desire to stage the Olympic Games in green spaces, since it was to be an event which would take up the cause of transparency and openness. The requirement of using as little material as possible suited the cantilevered tent roof developed by Frei Otto. The thin membrane structure covers an area of over 70,000 square meters. The transparent acrylic-glass-plate net stretches across the landscape and buildings, the western part of the Olympic Stadium, the Olympic Hall, and the Olympic Swim Hall. Deep concrete foundations and high-tension steel cables carry the main load of the construction; the roof net is supported by just twelve large pylons and thirty-six smaller round pillars. The project was also avant-garde in cost terms: the roof cladding cost one thousand percent more than was originally budgeted.

left—RENZO PIANO AND RICHARD ROGERS, CENTRE GEORGES POMPIDOU | Paris | 1971–77.

1971—Completion of the Aswan Dam · · · · · · · · · · · · · · · · · · · **1973**—Augusto Pinochet assumes power in Chile · · · · · · · · · · · · · ·

1974—Richard Nixon resigns · · · · · · · · · · · · · · · · ·

A building that ostentatiously shows off its infra-
structure and services is the Centre Georges Pompidou in Paris, which was built between 1971 and 1977.
Architects Richard Rogers (b. 1933) and Renzo Piano
(b. 1937) won the competition to create the cultural
center with a provocative design which has subse-
quently become the epitome of the high-tech style
(fig. p. 170). From the start Rogers and Piano refused
to make the project fit in with the historical architecture of the Place Beaubourg. On the contrary: they
built a futuristic complex of buildings right in the city
center. Working with the engineering studio of Ove
Arup & Partners, the architects developed a framework construction in which parts of the building and
its components could be installed at different points
in the construction and later replaced, according
to requirements. The building's articulation in
thirteen open bays surrounded by a steel framework
is highly visible. By housing all the structural and
service systems on the outside of the building, the
architects could make the interior into an ideal
exhibition space. Thus the Centre Pompidou boasts a
space of 170 x 48 meters unencumbered by supports.

right—**GÜNTER BEHNISCH AND FREI OTTO, OLYMPIC STADIUM**
Munich | 1968 – 72.

1980—Assassination of John Lennon ························· **1982**—Helmut Kohl becomes Chancellor of Germany·······························

1984—The Apple Macintosh is introduced ·······························

Its technology is present before the very eyes of passersby. Among the technical elements which are located on the outside are, for example, the round water-filled steel columns, which stand at regular intervals in front of the façade. In case of fire, the water circulates around the building, thus reducing the heat of the steel components. The service ducts on the outside, as well as the escalators, which move diagonally up the west façade, accentuate the building's façades with their primary colors: the water ducts are green, the escalator shafts red, electricity is shown in yellow, and the air-conditioning flows through blue tubes.

The headquarters of the Hongkong and Shanghai Bank in the center of Hong Kong is also a first in the story of high-tech architecture. The building was the first highrise design by British architect Norman Foster (1935–) (fig. above). The 180-meter-high block, which was completed in 1986, became the most expensive building in the world with building costs of five billion Hong Kong dollars. It is fundamentally different from the steel-and-glass highrise towers that surround it. Even the shape of the building is peculiar. Built on a rectangular ground-plan, the building is characterized vertically by the façade's three distinct backward steps, which break the tower down optically into segments. These four parts are also of different heights, which thus corresponded

with the architectural zoning of Hong Kong. On the west and east sides, service towers for equipment and emergency exit facilities are attached to the building. The steel construction lends the tower its horizontal articulation: individual floors are suspended without supports between monumental masts. Open working areas and large open spaces were part of the planning requirements, as were making good use of daylight and transparency. Foster achieved this on the main and rear façades by the use of floor-to-ceiling windows which frame views of the sea and The Peak. Unconventional materials are also a feature of high-tech architecture. Canadian architect Frank O. Gehry (b. 1929) employed an exotic material in the Spanish Basque region branch of the Guggenheim Museum, which was created between 1993 and 1997. The Guggenheim glistens in the port of Bilbao in an architecturally completely untypical way: its titanium skin changes its color gradations according to light conditions. But this material is not unknown: it is frequently used in particular in the aircraft industry. Several of the metal's properties make it seem

above—**NORMAN FOSTER, HONGKONG AND SHANGHAI BANK**
Hong Kong | 1979 – 86.

right—**FRANK O. GEHRY, GUGGENHEIM BILBAO** | 1993 – 97.

1986—Nuclear disaster in Chernobyl
1987—Ronald Reagan speaks in front of the Brandenburg Gate
1989—Fall of the Berlin Wall

HIGH-TECH **174/175**

"The Guggenheim Museum Bilbao glistens in a titanium skin – a material, used in particular in the aircraft industry."

highly suitable for architectural use as well: it is light, tough, and flexible and, unlike steel or aluminum, it does not corrode (fig. p. 175). The Guggenheim Bilbao is an extravagantly shaped building. It is surrounded by water which reflects the titanium surface of the building. In order to create Gehry's complex architectural shapes, his studio became pioneers in working with state-of-the-art computer simulation software that is otherwise used mainly in industry. To do this the computer determined the form of the titanium cladding's computer-aided manufacture and analysed the steel construction that would be needed to support it. While high-tech architects work closely with engineers, Santiago Calatrava from Spain combines both roles, engineer *and* architect, in one person. His bridges and numerous designs for public buildings demonstrate Calatrava's interest in technology and aesthetics. The TGV rail station at Satolas near Lyon was an important contribution to establishing Calatrava's reputation. The new station for France's network of high-speed trains looks like a giant

bird with a glass body and a concrete beak pointing to the ground, which forms the front of station (fig. p. 176 and above). However, Calatrava rejected any similarity with shapes from the animal world: "The 'beak' was formed as the result of complex calculations of the forces playing on the structure. It also happens to be the assembly point for the water run-off pipes. "Naturally, I did my best to minimize the mass of that point, without any thought of an anthropomorphic design." (Philip Jodidio, *Santiago Calatrava*, Taschen, 1998 p. 22) Not only is the 450-meter-long hall, which was completed in 1994, the high-speed train station; at the same time it also forms a link to Lyon's airport via an 180-meter-long steel bridge. The hall is lit by a row of lozenge-shaped overhead lights. The curved steel roof weighs 1,300 tonnes but still conveys the idea of dynamism effortlessly. And this is not all: it also aids passenger orientation. That was one of the most important demands made on the architects, as ultimately the Saint-Exupéry station is a meeting point of air, rail, and local traffic.

left and above—SANTIAGO CALATRAVA, TGV RAIL STATION, SATOLAS
Lyon | 1990 – 94.

1977—Jimmy Carter becomes President of the US .... **1980**—Assassination of John Lennon ....

1979—NATO Double-Track Decision ....

178/179

THE ADVENTURE OF DECONSTRUCTIVISM: FORM FOLLOWS FANTASY

Does a floor have to be horizontal? Or a wall vertical? The Deconstructivists answered these questions with a decisive "no," and were frequently met by the incomprehension of their audience in return. One of the main proponents of this style is architect Frank Gehry (b. 1929). Spectacular buildings such as his Guggenheim Museum in Bilbao make clear what Deconstructivism is all about: no backward glance, no imitation of old styles or forms, but the unequivocal search for new expressive possibilities. It also uses a wide palette of building materials, including many unusual ones, such as for example titanium which was used for the external cladding of the Guggenheim Bilbao (see fig. p. 175). A building's structure and equilibrium are called into question, as many of the finished buildings appear quite unfinished and occasionally look more like building sites than buildings ready for occupancy.

The Vitra Design Museum in Weil am Rhein, Germany, is another building which in its asymmetrically integrated forms calls into question established ways of seeing. Vitra, a furniture design

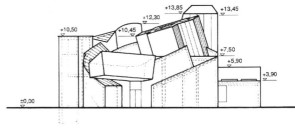

Ansicht von Nordosten.

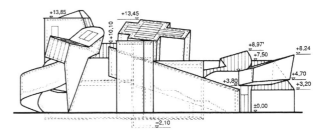

Ansicht von Nordwesten.

left—**FRANK O. GEHRY, VITRA DESIGN MUSEUM** | Weil am Rhein.
right—**VITRA DESIGN MUSEUM** | construction drawing.

180/181 DECONSTRUCTIVISM ···**1984**—The Apple Macintosh is introduced·· **1989**—Fall of the Berlin Wall

1986—Nuclear disaster in Chernobyl···

1987—Ronald Reagan speaks in front of the Brandenburg Gate··········

company, wanted to make its chair collection accessible to the public, and between 1987 and 1989 Frank Gehry created the building to do just that. This was also Gehry's first design for a building to be realized on European soil. The whitewashed building with its shining silver roofs is a collage of tilting towers, ramps, and cubes, and winding staircases which are piled one on top of the other in a way which is not as random as one might think. Rather, the function of its spaces and the direction of the light determined the expressive form of the exhibition center (fig. p. 178). Originally Gehry wanted to clad the exterior in sheet metal, "like an old oil can", as the architect described it. In the end, however, white plaster was used, and only the roof surfaces are covered in sheet metal. Like a sculpture, which allows the viewer to move around it, the Vitra Design Museum also offers completely different views according to the viewer's changing position. Depending on which side one approaches the building from, its image is determined by straight forms or curves, by triangles or cubes, pervaded by slanting, jagged, or meandering lines.

This matches the motto of Bernard Tschumi (b. 1944): "form follows fantasy"—of this the Swiss architect was certain. Here he was taking up the Modernist credo "form follows function" and then completely contradicting it. Tschumi and Gehry were among

the architects whose designs went on view at the 1988 exhibition, Deconstructivist Architecture. Through this show at the Museum of Modern Art in New York, curators Philip Johnson and Mark Wigley helped to bring this style to international attention. At MoMA Tschumi exhibited his design for the Parc de la Villette in Paris (fig. above and right). The project is characterized by its incompleteness, which was planned from the outset: three systems of points, lines, and surfaces overlap within the park. This allows sightlines to be broken down by fragments of buildings, buildings whose function remains a mystery. The circle is a constant form in the design, and it recurs in the park again and again, albeit taken apart or de-constructed. A series of bright red structures, each made up of different forms, have been randomly assigned a role. These 26 "follies" are most eye-catching because of their color contrast with the green of their surroundings. Many of the follies offer vantage points around the 55-hectare park; one is a studio, another a restaurant, and yet another serves as a welcome center for visitors. Ultimately the New York exhibition catalog on Deconstructivist

above—**BERNHARD TSCHUMI, PARC DE LA VILLETTE** | Paris | 1982–98.
right—**LA GÉODE IN THE PARC DE LA VILLETTE** | 1985.

*"Deconstructivism is all about:
no backward glance, no imitation of
old styles or forms, but the unequivocal
search for new expressive possibilities."*

2003—Beginning of the War in Iraq ·········· **DECONSTRUCTIVISM** **182/183**
2001—Terrorist attacks on World Trade Center ('9/11') ··········
2002—Introduction of the Euro··········

left—**PETER EISENMAN, WEXNER CENTER FOR THE VISUAL ARTS**
Columbus, Ohio | 1985–89.
right—**DANIEL LIBESKIND, JEWISH MUSEUM BERLIN** | 1989–98.

Architecture considered that Tschumi's park was a destabilization of pure architectural form. Instability could also be a key word for the designs of Peter Eisenman (b. 1932). In 1985 the American architect designed a building for Ohio State University, the Wexner Center. The structure itself does not seem to be entirely stable, as a white metal scaffolding sways between brick towers which look as though they have been sliced in two, and a tilted beam mediates between the wobbly parts of the building (fig. left). Eisenman had already engaged on a theoretical level with Deconstructivism, in particular with the work of the French philosopher Jacques Derrida (1930–2004). He regarded traditional notions of architecture, whether classical or modern, with skepticism. The dismantling of old structures and forms are at the forefront of his work of translating the complex ideas of philosophical Deconstructivism into architecture. A white grid structure runs the entire length of the building, but this is pushed to one side of the main axis of the building complex and seems an alien element, particularly as its specific function remains unclear. And this theme continues: columns and beams peter out in space, and windows are inserted into the floor. The Wexner Center is far removed from traditional notions of construction. Even the entrance area with its slender brick towers questions the function and form of architectural structures more than it offers a clear statement.

Slanting wall, empty rooms with no apparent way out, asymmetrical stories, and dead ends also determine the form of another first in architectural Deconstructivism. The plan for the Jewish Museum in Berlin by Daniel Libeskind (b. 1946) existed well before the fall of the Berlin Wall, but it was only completed in 1999 (figs. pp. 183–185). From the outside the new building is characterized by sharp edges and its silvery sheen. The extension to the historical museum in the Kreuzberg district of Berlin is clad with gray sheets of zinc and pierced with slit-shaped strip windows. Its ground-plan is in the shape of a zigzag,

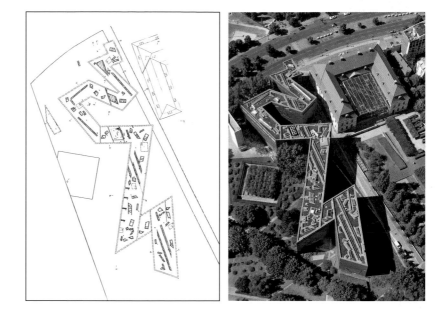

the architect's reference to the Star of David (fig. above). The jagged forms of the ground-plan proceed along a straight axis, and five empty rooms, the "Voids", form the interfaces between both lines. These rooms with bare concrete walls are far removed from the usual idea of a room since, apart from one exception, they are inaccessible. The Voids are intended to represent architecturally the emptiness that remains after the Holocaust. Three underground axes, their floors inclined in places and with an ingenious lighting system, lead to the various main themes of the exhibition. The "Axis of Emigration", for example, directs the visitor via an increasingly narrow corridor between slightly slanting walls, and finally out into the open air. The architect's own description of his design for the Berlin Museum addressed its contradictory and uncompromising nature: "The Jewish Museum is conceived as an emblem in which the Invisible and the Visible are the structural features which have been gathered in this space of Berlin and laid bare in an architecture where the unnamed remains the name which keeps still." (Bernhard Schneider, *Daniel Libeskind, Jewish Museum Berlin: Between the Lines*, Prestel 1999, p. 6)

left—**Jewish Museum Berlin** | interior view.
above left—**Jewish Museum Berlin** | ground plan.
above right—**Jewish Museum Berlin** | aerial view.
next double page spread—**Zaha Hadid, Bridge Pavilion** | Zaragoza 2005–08.

LIST OF ARCHITECTS

Filippo **Brunelleschi**: born 1377 in Florence;
died April 15, 1446 in Florence

Leon Battista **Alberti**: born February 14, 1404 in Genoa;
died April 1472 in Rome

Donato **Bramante**: born 1444 in Monte Asdrualdo bei
Fermignano/Pesaro; died April 11, 1514 in Rome

Michelangelo **Buonarroti**: born March 6, 1475 in
Caprese; died February 18, 1564 in Rome

Sebastiano **Serlio**: born September 6, 1475 in Bologna;
died between 1553 and 1555 in Fontainebleau

Andrea **Palladio**: born November 8, 1508 in Padua;
died August 19, 1580 in Vicenza

Carlo **Maderno**: born 1555 or 1556 in Capolago near
Lugano; died January 31, 1629 in Rome

Gian Lorenzo **Bernini**: born December 7, 1598 in Naples;
died November 28, 1680 in Rome

Francesco **Borromini**: born September 27, 1599 in Bisso-
ne/Lake Lugano; died August 2, 1667 in Rome

Louis **Le Vau**: born 1612 in Paris; died October 11,
1670 in Paris

Jules Hardouin **Mansart**: born April 16, 1646 in Paris;
died May 8, 1708 in Paris

Matthäus Daniel **Pöppelmann**: born May 3, 1662 in
Herford; died January 17, 1736 in Dresden

Carl Gotthard **Langhans**: born December 15, 1732 in
Landeshut, Silesia (today Poland);
died October 1, 1808 in Wroclaw, Poland

Abraham **Darby**: born 1750 in Shropshire; died 1789

Pierre-Alexandre **Vignon**: born October 5, 1763 in Lagny;
died May 21, 1828 in Paris

Joseph **Paxton**: born August 3, 1803 in Milton-Bryant,
Bedfordshire; died June 8, 1865 in Sydenham

Giuseppe **Mengoni**: born November 2, 1829 in Fontana
Elice near Ravenna; died December 30, 1877 in Milan

William LeBaron **Jenney**: born September 25, 1832
in Fairhaven, Massachusetts; died June 15, 1907
in Los Angeles

Daniel H. **Burnham**: born September 4, 1846 in
Henderson, New York; died June 1, 1912 in Heidelberg

Gustave **Eiffel**: born December 15, 1832 in Dijon;
died December 27, 1923 in Paris

Frank Lloyd **Wright**: born June 8, 1867 in Richland
Center, Wisconsin; died April 9, 1959 in Phoenix,
Arizona

Max **Berg**: born April 17, 1870 in Szczecin;
died January 24, 1947 in Baden-Baden

Auguste **Perret**: born February 12, 1874 in Brussels;
died February 25, 1954 in Paris

Adolf **Meyer**: born June 17, 1881 in Mechernich near
Euskirchen; died July 24, 1929 in Baltrum, East Frisia

William **van Alen**: born August 10, 1882 in Brooklyn,
New York; died May 24, 1954 in New York

Pierre **Chareau**: born August 3, 1883 in Bordeaux;
died 1950 in East Hampton, New York

Walter **Gropius**: born May 18, 1883 in Berlin;
died July 5, 1969 in Boston

Ludwig Mies **van der Rohe**: born March 27, 1886 in
Aachen; died August 17, 1969 in Chicago

Le Corbusier (Charles-Edouard Jeanneret):
born October 6, 1887 in La Chaux-de-Fonds; died
August 27, 1965 in Roquebrune-Cap-Martin

Erich **Mendelsohn**: born March 21, 1887 in Allenstein,
East Prussia; died September 15, 1953 in
San Francisco

Ove **Arup**: born April 16, 1895 in Newcastle upon Tyne;
died January 29, 1988 in London

Alvar **Aalto**: born February 3, 1898 in Kuortane;
died May 11, 1976 in Helsinki

Philip **Johnson**: born July 8, 1906 in Cleveland, Ohio;
died January 15, 2005 in New Canaan, Connecticut

Günther **Behnisch**: born June 12, 1922 in Lockwitz near
Dresden; died July 12, 2010 in Stuttgart

Oscar **Niemeyer**: born December 15, 1907 in
Rio de Janeiro

Eero **Saarinen**: born August 20, 1910 in
Kirkkonummi, Finland; died September 1, 1961 in
Ann Arbor, Michigan

Kenzo **Tange**: born September 4, 1913 in Osaka; died
March 22, 2005 in Tokyo

Ieoh **Ming Pei**: born April 26, 1917 in Guangzhou, China

Jørn **Utzon**: born April 9, 1918 in Copenhagen; died
September 29, 2008 near Copenhagen

Frei **Otto**: born May 31, 1925 in Sigmar, today Chemnitz

Frank O. **Gehry**: born February 28, 1929 in Toronto

Peter **Eisenman**: born August 11, 1932 in Newark,
New Jersey

Richard **Rogers**: born July 27, 1933 in Florence

Norman **Foster**: born June 1, 1935 in Manchester

Renzo **Piano**: born September 14, 1937 in Genoa

Rafael **Moneo**: born May 9, 1937 in Tudela, Navarra

Bernhard **Tschumi**: born January 25, 1944 in Lausanne

Jean **Nouvel**: born August 20, 1945 in Fumel, France

Daniel **Libeskind**: born May 12, 1946 in Lodz, Poland

Santiago **Calatrava**: born July 28, 1951 in Valencia

SELECTED BIBLIOGRAPHY

ADDIS, BILL. *Building: 3,000 Years of Design, Engineering and Construction.* London, 2007.

BINDING, GÜNTHER. *Als die Kathedralen in den Himmel wuchsen. Bauen im Mittelalter.* Darmstadt, 2006.

BLAU, EVE AND MONIKA PLATZER (eds.). *Shaping the Great City. Modern Architecture in Central Europe 1890–1937.* Munich, 1999.

BRACE TAYLOR, BRIAN. *Pierre Chareau: Designer and Architect.* Cologne, 1992.

COSSONS, NEIL AND BARRIE TRINDER. *The Iron Bridge: Symbol of the Industrial Revolution.* Wiltshire, 1979.

DAVIES, COLIN. *High-Tech Architecture.* London, 1988.

DUPRÉ, JUDITH. *Skyscrapers.* New York, 1996.

EMANUEL, MURIEL (ed.). *Contemporary Architects.* Detroit, 1994.

ENGELS, HANS. *Bauhaus Architecture.* Munich, 2001.

FAJARDO, JULIO. *Hi-Tec Architecture.* Cologne, 2010.

FRAMPTON, KENNETH. *Modern Architecture: A Critical History.* London, 1980.

HART, FRANZ. *Kunst und Technik der Wölbung.* Munich, 1965.

ISAACS, REGINALD. *Gropius: An Illustrated Biography of the Bauhaus.* Boston, 1991.

JORDY, WILLIAM H. *American Buildings and Their Architects: The Impact of European Modernism in the Mid-Twentieth Century.* New York/Oxford, 1972.

KLOTZ, HEINRICH. *The History of Post-modern Architecture.* Cambridge, Mass., 1988.

KOHLMAIER, GEORG AND BARNA VON SARTORY. *Houses of Glass: A Nineteenth-century Building Type.* Trans. John C. Harvey. Cambridge, 1986.

PEVSNER, NIKOLAUS, HUGH HONOUR, AND JOHN FLEMING. *Penguin Dictionary of Architecture and Landscape Architecture.* Harmondsworth, 2000.

REICHOLD, KLAUS AND BERNHARD GRAF. *Buildings that Changed the World.* Munich, 1999.

SCHILDT-GÖRAN. *Alvar Aalto: The Master Works.* New York, 1998.

THIEL-SILING, SABINE (ED.). *Icons of Architecture: the 20th Century.* Munich, 2005.

THOMSON, CHRISTIAN W. VISIONARY ARCHITECTURE: *From Babylon to Virtual Reality.* Munich, 1994.

TRACHTENBERG, MARCIN AND ISABELLE HYMAN. *Architecture from Prehistory to Post-modernism. The Western Tradition.* New York, 1986.

Exhibition Catalogues

ANDREAS, PAUL ET AL. (eds.), *Oscar Niemeyer. Eine Legende der Moderne* (exh. cat. Deutsches Architektur Museum, Frankfurt am Main, March 1 to November 5, 2003), Basel, 2003.

BRÜDERLIN, MARKUS (ed.), *ArchiSkulptur. Dialoge zwischen Architektur und Plastik vom 18. Jahrhundert bis heute* (exh. cat. Fondation Beyeler, Riehen/Basel, October 3, 2004 to January 30, 2005), Ostfildern, 2005.

FAGIOLO, MARCELLO (ed.), *Roma barocca* (exh. cat. Museo Nazionale di Castel Sant'Angelo, Rome, June 16 to October 29, 2006), Milan, 2006.

JOHNSON, PHILIP AND MARK WIGLEY (eds.), *Deconstructivist Architecture* (exh. cat. Museum of Modern Art, New York, June 23 to August 30, 1988), New York, 1988.

MILLON, HENRY A. AND CRAIG HUGH SMYTH, (eds.), *Michelangelo Architect. The Facade of San Lorenzo and the Drum and Dome of St. Peter's* (exh. cat. National Gallery of Art, Washington, October 9 to December 11, 1988), Milan, 1988.

RAEBURN, MICHAEL (ed.), *Le Corbusier. Architect of the Century* (exh. cat. Hayward Gallery, London, March 5 to June 7, 1987), London, 1987.

INDEX

Numbers in *italics* refer to images.

PHOTO CREDITS

akg-images: 26; 34 (Rabatti-Dominghie); 44, 91 (Andrea Jemolo); 46/47, 184
(Bildarchiv Monheim); 54 r (Stefan Drechsel); 61, 65 (Erich Lessing);
97 (Hervé Champollion); 105 (IAM); 128 (Hilbich); 136, 183 (Florian Profit-
lich); 150, 178 (Schütze / Rodemann); 170 (Electa); 185 r (euroluftbild.de)
Archives nationales/Institut français d'architecture, Fonds Perret: 153
Bauhaus-Archiv Berlin: 144 r
Achim Bednorz, Cologne: 23, 43, 74, 75, 100
Bildagentur Huber, GAP / Giovanni Simeone: 37
Bilderberg, Hamburg / Reinhart Wolf: 85
Hervé Champollion: 17
Chicago Historical Society, Chicago: 116 l
S. Chirol: 54 l
Helge Classen: 138 r
CORBIS, Düsseldorf / Richard Hamilton Smith: 118
Hans Engels: 134, 137, 139
Esto, Mamaroneck, NY / Peter Mauss: 114, 117
Michael Freeman: 166/167
getty: 10 (WILL & DENI MCINTYRE), 12/13 (Ravi Tahilramani), 20 (Fergus
O'Brien), 33 (Tetra Images), 48 (Leemage), 55 (Dennis Barnes),
80 (DEA/A. DE GREGORIO), 86 (James L. Stanfield), 89 (Gamma-Rapho via
Getty Images), 92/93 (Eurasia), 101 (Ingolf Pompe), 106/107 (John Lamb),
109 (SSPL via Getty Images), 110/111 (Panoramic Images), 122 (Buena Vista
Images), 124/125 (TC Lin), 142 (Walter Bibikow), 155 (Mark R. Thomas),
159 (Christophe Lehenaff), 168 (Time & Life Pictures/Getty Images),
180 (Arnaud Chicurel), 181 (Olivier Colas)
Jeff Goldberg/Esto: 182
Markus Hilbich: 51
Angelo Hornak: 120, 121 l u. r
Japan-Photo-Archiv: 158
Rainer Kiedrowski: 83, 172/173
Atelier Klaus Kinold: 141
laif: 2 (Stefan Falke), 9 (ChinaFotoPress), 19 (Mattes René/hemis.fr), 30 (Zanettini),
38/39 (Sasse), 40 (Gerhard Westrich), 52 (Galli), 62/63 (Emile Luider/Rapho),
81 , 98/99 (Kirchner), 113, 132/133 (Eddie Gerald), 145 (Prignet/Le Figaro
Magazine), 148/149 (Digaetano/Polaris), 152 (Samuel Zuder), 154 (Pierre-
Olivier Deschamps/VU), 164, 169 (Mark Fiennes/Arcaid), 186/187 (Benoit
DECOUT/REA)
Ian Lambot: 174
Alexander Langkals, Landshut: 78/79
LOOK: Cover (age fotostock), 16
Norman McGrath: 129
Gerhard Murza: 160
Cathleen Naundorf: 157
Ralph Richter/Architekturphoto: 176, 177
Christian Richters Fotograf: 175
Philippe Rualt, Nantes: 147
Jordi Sarrá: 130
Stadtplanungsamt Stuttgart: 138 l
Stiftung Archiv der Akademie der Künste, Berlin: 126
The Art Institute of Chicago, J. W. Taylor Photographer: 116 r
Jussi Tiainen: 140
Nigel Young, Foster and Partners: 131
Alfred Wolf: 15

IMPRINT

© Prestel Verlag, Munich · London · New York, 2012
© for the works reproduced is held by the architects and artists, their heirs
or assigns, with the exception of: Santiago Calatrava, Walter Gropius and
Frank Lloyd Wright with VG Bild-Kunst, Bonn 2012

Front cover: Frank Lloyd Wright, *Solomon R. Guggenheim Museum* | 1943–59 |
view of the cupola.
Back cover: (from left to right) *Flatiron Building*, see p. 114; Santiago Calatrava,
Auditorio de Tenerife, see p. 159; Walter Gropius with Adolf Meyer, *Bauhaus*,
staircase, see p. 134
Frontispiece: César Pelli, *World Financial Center* | New York | 1985–88 | detail.

Prestel Verlag, Munich
A member of Verlagsgruppe Random House GmbH

Prestel Verlag
Neumarkter Strasse 28
81673 Munich
Tel. +49 (0)89 4136-0
Fax +49 (0)89 4136-2335

Prestel Publishing Ltd.
4 Bloomsbury Place
London WC1A 2QA
Tel. +44 (0)20 7323-5004
Fax +44 (0)20 7636-8004

Prestel Publishing
900 Broadway, Suite 603
New York, NY 10003
Tel. +1 (212) 995-2720
Fax +1 (212) 995-2733

www.prestel.com

Library of Congress Control Number is available; British Library Cataloguing-
in-Publication Data: a catalogue record for this book is available from the British
Library; Deutsche Nationalbibliothek holds a record of this publication in the
Deutsche Nationalbibliografie; detailed bibliographical data can be found under:
http://dnb.d-nb.de

Prestel books are available worldwide. Please contact your nearest bookseller or
one of the above addresses for information concerning your local distributor.

Translated by: Philippa Hurd, London
Editorial direction: Claudia Stäuble and Julie Kiefer
Copyedited by: Jane Michael, Munich
Picture editor: Franziska Stegmann
Timelines and index: Andrea Jaroni
Cover design: Joana Niemeyer, April
Design: LIQUID Agentur für Gestaltung, Augsburg
Layout: Stephan Riedlberger, Munich
Production: Astrid Wedemeyer
Art direction: Cilly Klotz
Origination: ReproLine Mediateam, München
Printing and binding: Druckerei Uhl GmbH & Co. KG, Radolfzell

Printed in Germany

ISBN 978-3-7913-4654-0
(German edition: ISBN 978-3-7913-4655-7)